OPPOSING THE SYSTEM

OPPOSING THE SYSTEM

CHARLES A. REICH

CROWN PUBLISHERS, INC. NEW YORK

Copyright © 1995 by Charles A. Reich

Published by Crown Publishers, Inc., 201 East 50th Street, New York, New York 10022. Member of the Crown Publishing Group.

Random House, Inc. New York, Toronto, London, Sydney, Auckland

CROWN is a trademark of Crown Publishers, Inc.

Manufactured in the United States of America

Design by June Bennett-Tantillo

Library of Congress Cataloging-in-Publication Data

Reich, Charles A.
    Opposing the system / Charles A. Reich.—1st ed.
        p.   cm.
    1. United States—Social conditions—1980– 2.United States—
Politics and government—1989–   3. Protest movements—United
States.   I. Title.
    HN59.2.R438   1995
306'.0973—dc20   95-24249
                                                                        CIP

ISBN 0-517-59777-2

10   9   8   7   6   5   4   3   2   1

First Edition

TO MY DEAR FRIEND BEATRICE BOWLES

CONTENTS

Contents

ACKNOWLEDGMENTS

Greg Marriner talked through the ideas of the book with me; served as a research, editorial, and writing assistant; and typed and retyped the manuscript. To all of these demanding tasks he brought professionalism and extraordinary dedication. Greg, who also worked on *The Sorcerer of Bolinas Reef* (1976), has been a longtime and indispensable source of support, a task in which he is now joined by his wife, Karen, and son, Max.

Yale Law School has been my intellectual home for forty-five years, and many of the ideas in this book owe their origin to the school's unique atmosphere. I am grateful to Judge Guido Calabresi, the former dean, and to Dean Anthony T. Kronman for extending the school's hospitality to me in the years when I was writing this book. The following friends and colleagues read earlier versions of the manuscript and were most generous with their time, suggestions, and individual points of view: Bruce Ackerman, Akhil Amar, Steven Duke, Joseph Goldstein, Burke Marshall, and John Simon. A special note of thanks for the "bad weather dinners" with Bruce Ackerman. Thanks also to three student assistants who made significant contributions to the book: Michelle Anderson, Anna Barber, and Robin Kelsey. I am grateful to Marcia Mayfield, Diane Milano, and Lynn Murinson for typing the manuscript and contributing their thoughts during my various stays at Yale. Ruth Emerson also read the manuscript and gave me the valued perspective of a longtime friend.

In San Francisco, Stephanie Wildman, my friend and former colleague at the University of San Francisco School of Law, also read the manuscript and contributed her ideas.

Steve Harrick, a Yale College senior at the time, served as a student assistant and helped me to get started on the earliest typed version of the book by taking dictation, providing feedback, and participating in a continuing conversation. He made a substantial contribution to the book's content.

I want to thank my editors, Richard Marek and Betty A. Prashker, for making suggestions which resulted in an immense improvement in the book's organization and clarity. My agent, Gerard McCauley, shepherded the book through its most perilous passage, and has been the author's good friend as well as an insightful critic.

There is no Wealth but Life. . . .

That country is the richest which nourishes the greatest number of noble and happy human beings.
                    —John Ruskin
          Unto This Last (1862)[1]

OPPOSING
THE
SYSTEM

1

AMERICA'S SEARCH FOR CHANGE

Discontent has become a powerful force in American life. The desire for change comes not only from the margins of society but straight from the heart of the middle class. As expressed in the 1994 election, the force of change has been described as an earthquake, a tidal wave, a revolution. Its concerns are profound: that democracy is not working and people feel powerless; that the economy forces most people into a losing struggle where earnings can never catch up to expenses; that rising social conflict is destroying safety and security; and that we have lost the ability to imagine a better future.

In response to this cry of pain we have seen the victory of those who would lead us back toward the pre–New Deal past. Apart from them, there is an extraordinary silence. Where are the voices of progress, of betterment, of hope? The main progressive ideas of this century have seemingly all been abandoned, and those who once had faith in these ideas appear ashamed, apologetic, and ready to recant. The silence of our thinkers reveals a crisis deeper than discontent—a failure of human intelligence to understand and master the unknown malady that threatens us. If we cannot explain the problem, we cannot fix it or cure it. So long as we cannot see what is wrong, we will have no valid new ideas or visions.

The present wave of protest is the latest chapter in a thirty-year search for change that has already assumed many forms and experimented with many different remedies. The 1992 election of Bill Clinton was also a vote for change; so was the vote for Ronald Reagan and, before that, for Jimmy Carter. Indeed, it is remarkable to recall how the wave of protest that marked the sixties carried the same message as conservatism does today; it is the remedies that differ. The Republicans talk about "more freedom." So did the hippies. The same is true of "too much coercion and control over our lives." Conservatives see a loss of traditional values; the sixties was a rebellion against dehumanization—also a loss of values. The sixties advocated personal responsibility and brought an end to a war by responsible individual action. The sixties was far ahead of conservatives in denouncing elitist liberalism, in demanding an end to violence, and in seeking a renewal of spiritual life.

Most important, sixties protest and nineties conservatism are both best understood as *responses*. They were and are responses to *unwanted change*—responses to a malady with many symptoms, all of which reflect the rise of impersonal oppression and a loss of the chance to flourish as human beings. If we put aside the extreme differences of style and outlook, we see people struggling against an unseen enemy, blaming the nearest source of frustration, and whether motivated by love or anger equally unable to bring about the changes they desire. We are all pressed downward by forces we cannot see or control. We are all stumbling in the dark.

There is a very real danger that those now in control will drive us straight off a cliff. Undeterred by mounting evidence of impending social catastrophe, they may bring about such dangerous inequality, such widespread insecurity, and such massive damage to the natural and human habitat that the deprived and dispossessed will wreak havoc in return. There may be no existing leadership or institutions which can be depended on to stop the juggernaut. What are the trapped passengers to do?

The next stage of this drama must inevitably be the return of protest, of demonstrations and direct action, as more and more people suffer harm and are unable to obtain redress from those in charge. But will the protestors repeat the mistakes made by earlier protestors, whose efforts, however passionate, were ultimately unsuccessful? Successful protest must be based upon an investigation and understanding of why previous protest failed. No matter how powerful our impatience to take action, we must pause long enough to see why action has thus far been ineffective.

In April 1995 the nation was shocked by the bombing of the federal building in Oklahoma City. In the aftermath, most people learned for the first time about paramilitary groups and individuals with an intense hatred and fear of the federal government. These groups cannot be dismissed as merely paranoid and crazy. They are correct in sensing that something is profoundly wrong. Unfortunately, their diagnosis of the problem is largely mistaken, and their means of expressing opposition are ineffectual at best, and tragically wrong when the result is violence and the loss of many innocent lives. But we must quickly find means of protest and reform that are both effective and positive.

If we are to escape our present downward and destructive course, we must learn from the failure of past efforts at reform, revolution, and renewal. We need an adequate theory of social change. We need to diagnose the malady that afflicts our society, and on the basis of that diagnosis, we need to fashion an appropriate remedy. We need a strategy that understands the obstacles that have been placed in the way of change—a strategy that can overcome these obstacles.

We need a believable and feasible alternative to the status quo that would represent the future rather than the past.

In the long run, we are going to need a science of social change. We have applied scientific knowledge to virtually all of the practical areas of life except government and economics—two areas still dominated by myths and ideology. If our economic and political institutions become dysfunctional, we will need to create a new area of knowledge to deal more intelligently with human affairs.

Our present efforts at change have been thwarted by a gigantic deception. The true causes of our problems have succeeded in remaining invisible, leaving us to fight the wrong enemies, often each other. Our anger and our energies are tragically misdirected. We are fighters who cannot find the enemy even as we suffer its blows. For thirty years this deception has succeeded, but at ever greater cost.

All of the efforts to achieve change so far represent an effort to adjust the relationship between two entities—citizens and government. But these efforts, whether they swing "left" or "right," are doomed to failure if they ignore the presence of a third entity— *economic government*. Citizens and public government together cannot change the direction of the country if both have ceded power over that direction to economic government. For despite appearances, public government, no matter how big, has actually *lost* a great deal of power in recent decades. Fewer and fewer important decisions are made through the political process. Citizens and government alike have lost power even as they struggle with each other. Economic government has absorbed power from both citizens *and* public government.

Economic government is a new phenomenon which arrived by stealthy means and has attracted little recognition or discussion. Yet its effects are everywhere and its presence changes both the nature of citizenship and the nature of public government. It has primary power over the very issues which are the source of today's discontent—such as the lower and lower value of most people's work. And economic government is by far the most important agent of social change—especially unwanted change, such as the growing insecurity that we all feel. Americans who hope that by reducing public government there will be an increase in individual freedom will find that "freedom" to be an illusion.

Moreover, economic government has changed the character of economic growth from a benefit to all to something utterly different in character—beneficial to some, extremely harmful to others. Economic growth is the true source of the conflicts that are tearing this country apart, because it is borrowing from and depleting the noneconomic side of life, a side that includes the welfare of the human beings who make up the workforce. Today, economic growth may be premised on forcing wages down to save costs, excluding an ever larger number of people from the workforce in the name of efficiency, imposing costs on those least able to pay, and undermining rather than supporting those "noneconomic" values such as family which both political parties claim to support. Today's "growth" promotes inequality, division, and impoverishment, not just improvement. The attempt to solve our economic and social problems while ignoring the existence of economic government is common to Republicans, Democrats, libertarians, economists, pundits, New Age philosophers, and the public. But if, despite our denials, economic government has become an essential component of our system, then we must confront that fact in order to regain control of our society.

By ignoring the decisive influence of economic government and its two-edged form of growth, we have been prey to simplistic explanations for profound problems—a current list of which might include:

- big government
- drugs
- violence in films and television
- absence of compulsory prayer in schools
- a culture of excessive permissiveness
- failure of personal responsibility

- decline of the work ethic
- guns
- absent fathers
- lenient treatment of criminals
- illegitimacy
- rock and rap lyrics
- schools not teaching basic values
- politicians
- the sixties counterculture
- welfare dependency
- not enough police
- not enough prison cells
- not enough death sentences

If the present Republican agenda fails to make a positive difference in people's lives, we will no doubt soon be seeking answers elsewhere. The public is extremely volatile and uncertain, ready to shift its loyalties from one program or leadership to another and then to shift again when promises and hopes prove disappointing. In its latest incarnation, the search for change has been interpreted as a mandate against "big government." But the "mandate" is a shaky one; many more people refrained from voting than actually participated in the 1994 election. What will we do if the pendulum keeps swinging but conditions continue to grow worse?

The political clamor and the battle to escape and

impose blame have distracted us from a disinterested search for causes and solutions. This search should now be placed at the top of our national agenda. When the forces of discontent cannot find an outlet and cannot see where they are going, a dangerous situation is created. People will accept simplistic answers that may make things much worse. The opportunity for dialogue and reason may be lost in a destructive surge of anger. Fear and repression may plunge us downward. Therefore it is urgent that we look beyond the immediate concerns of the discontented to ask where and how we lost the way.

As soon as we attempt to understand our society's underlying malady, we are confronted by a mystery—a detective story with much of the evidence hidden from sight. Since World War II, America has suffered a steady impoverishment that contradicts the official picture of glowing economic health. We see this impoverishment in our decaying cities, in the insecurity of our lives, in the deadly plague of homelessness, in the disappearance of money to pay for essential human needs like schools. Where has all the money gone? Why is there no money to pay for the upkeep of parks, libraries, schools, museums, and the other amenities and necessities of community life? Not so long ago there was money for all of these things. Supposedly, our country has grown much richer in recent decades. How can this economic growth be reconciled with our inability to find money for needs that were once taken for granted? Our national, state, and city governments are all impoverished today. Private institutions are cutting back as well. What is the explanation?

When confronted by a mystery which has resisted all conventional efforts at a solution, human beings need not feel defeated and powerless. We have another choice. Human beings have the power to question their own assumptions.

Today, most of us lack an intelligible picture of our world. We know that our government and economy no longer fit the models we were taught in school. We know that our efforts to influence government and the economy as voters, consumers, and workers fail to bring the responses we would expect from a free-market democracy. Even those whose careers are headed toward public life cannot map the structure they plan to enter.

As members of society, we assume that we possess an accurate picture of our institutions and how they function. We look to the Constitution, the free market, and the principles of democracy as our guidelines. But without our knowledge, these landmarks have been altered so that our assumptions concerning them are no longer valid. Our society no longer works the way it is supposed to. We find ourselves in the position of the baffled child in a dysfunctional family. We are burdened with a *false map of reality*. And like any other inaccurate map, it misleads rather than helps us.

A false map of reality is one aspect of a larger malfunction that might be called *lack of social self-knowledge*. We know that we can all be subject to lack of personal self-knowledge. This condition can and often does mislead and misinform us at every moment of decision or choice. What we need to imagine is a similar lack of knowledge of ourselves as a society, a lack of *social self-knowledge*. We fail to understand the larger organism or structure of which we are a part. We lack insight into how and why it acts, how and why it treats us as it does, what it cares about, what its rules, if any, are. If the absence of personal self-knowledge may be compared to stumbling in the dark, lack of social self-knowledge means an even more frightening necessity of navigating through life without rules or directions.

There are many reasons why we might lose knowledge of our own society. Much of what we know about our world is secondhand, something we are told, rather than something we experience firsthand. We rely on others to tell us how government works, how the economy works. Moreover, the sources of our knowledge are the government and other large institutions, not observers with an outside point of view. But the chief reason for erroneous knowledge of reality is rapid social change that makes existing knowledge, no matter how obtained, obsolete.

Societies change in more than one way. We are familiar with *intentional social change,* the kind represented by the Declaration of Independence and the New Deal, the kind we have been unable to achieve in recent decades. But there is another and far more potent form of change: *unintended social change*—such as the rise of crime and violence or the increasing insecurity of the middle class. It is important to divide unintended social change into two categories: that which is recognized and acknowledged, even if it is not desired—such as urban decay or automobile pollution—and that which is unrecognized and unacknowledged. What we are aware of, we can deal with. What we are unaware of can deceive us and cause our best efforts to be misdirected.

It is the category of unacknowledged social change that helps to explain the mystery. For example, if we picture our society as a place where economic opportunity is open to all who are willing and able to work, when in fact there are no longer enough good jobs for those who seek them, the shortage of jobs and the consequent loss of economic opportunity represents *unacknowledged social change.* When our thinking fails to keep up with changed conditions, we suffer from *lag.* The greater the lag in our thinking, the more mistakes we will make and the more dysfunctional our actions will become.

Thus it is possible that our institutions have been

fundamentally changed without our knowledge. Indeed, the possibility of such an unwanted transformation might have been foreseen. Our nation was
founded, and its Constitution written, before the age of
technology, before the age of large organizations, before the effects of the industrial revolution had become
apparent. The immense forces created by organization
and technology are in many ways based on principles
inconsistent with democracy and constitutional government. It should be no surprise that these forces
have profoundly altered both our constitutional democracy and our free economy.

Loss of social self-knowledge gives rise to the phenomenon of *invisibility*. Today, much of the system by
which we are governed is invisible, because it is either
not seen at all or seen incorrectly. The system that we
"see" is democracy and a free market. But if we really
have such a system, why have the people's efforts at
change failed over and over again? The answer is that
we are actually governed by a system we cannot see—an
invisible system. In order to develop ideas about what
has gone wrong and how things could change for the
better, we must first see this invisible system.

We must attempt to imagine a picture of our government and economy that explains all of the phenomena of our social world, including its failure to function
as it is supposed to, and the mysteries of powerlessness, lack of democracy, impoverishment despite eco-

nomic growth, and loss of America's dream. We must
try to create a picture of reality that makes logical sense
of the rise of crime and violence, the disappearance of
economic security, the growing disparity between rich
and poor, the gradual descent toward "third world status," and the persistence and growth of a permanent
underclass.

In attempting to repicture reality, we must also
seek to show what has happened to our hopes. Every
generation of Americans has had its dreams. What has
prevented their fulfillment? Where are the Four Freedoms, including freedom from want and freedom from
fear, described by President Franklin D. Roosevelt as
the goals of World War II? Where is the ideal of a
society based on love, caring, and community that the
pioneers of the sixties pictured? Where is the "city on a
hill" that Ronald Reagan imagined? Where is the "society that puts people first" that Bill Clinton promised?
What has prevented these hopes from being realized,
and where may they yet be found?

The invisible system that governs us has no name.
It represents a combination of two kinds of government—public government and private economic government, functioning together. This combined system
has escaped all traditional limits and controls. It has
circumvented the Constitution, nullified democracy,
and overridden the free market. It usurps our powers
and dominates our lives. Yet we cannot see it or de-

scribe it. It is new to human history. It is immensely powerful but without brakes, indifferent to the effect of its actions on human beings.

There is no imposing marble building in Washington, D.C., with "THE SYSTEM" carved across its portico. The System is a merger of governmental, corporate, and media power into a managerial entity more powerful by reason of technology, organization, and control of livelihood than any previously known form of rule.

To describe the System in this way must inevitably sound alarmist. But before dismissing this picture, remember how powerless most people feel. Ordinary people feel no ability to influence the decay, the violence, the insecurity that threatens their lives. Even those in high places have no control over what is happening to our society. Our experience of helplessness contradicts the image of a democracy subject to law and to the will of the people. Our stress, anger, and frustration do not square with the conventional picture of a market that is responsive to our needs and desires. Our fear of the future does not accord with the premise that we are in charge, that the society obeys our will. Instead, we feel like terrified passengers on a careening, off-course airliner or train.

The System represents a higher level of decision-making at which choices affecting us all are made. We need to see this higher level in order to have any effective influence upon it. In the drama of our times, the System is the missing actor in the show—with the biggest part. Inability to discern the System's functioning represents an intellectual failure by economists, political scientists, and legal scholars, whose incomplete assumptions about reality mislead them. If the System seems like an alien power out of science fiction, that is because it is so different from what we have known in the past.

The System has inevitably rejected more and more of the eighteenth-century constitutional and economic vision. Technology and organization emphasize control rather than freedom of economic opportunity, and the System these forces have joined to produce has predictably rejected both constitutional and market freedoms to become a law unto itself. The System has given us many benefits, but its hidden costs and failures are now being revealed. It has been increasingly unable or unwilling to include everyone in the prosperity that is its main justification. More and more of what the System calls economic growth has proven to be a depletion of fundamental values. Dehumanization and damage to human beings are side effects of the System's operations. As these pathologies have become more acute, the System has resorted to blame and repression rather than reform. It is now producing a slow but overwhelming social and economic catastrophe that threatens to engulf us all.

At the heart of this catastrophe is the loss of the individual's power over livelihood. Livelihood includes the right to work, the ability to make a living, the opportunity to participate in society. Slowly but inexorably we have lost control over this most basic of all human necessities. It is the System which now controls the right of livelihood, and in its indifference to individual human beings it treats many people as surplus, others as disposable or of little value, and everyone else as if their interests and happiness matter only to the extent that they are useful to the System. Poverty, layoffs, falling wages, temporary employment without benefits, and lack of meaning in work are some of the harmful consequences of the loss of power over livelihood. As people lose power over livelihood, they are forced to accept a loss of democracy as well. Technology and organization prefer an authoritarian workplace to a democratic one. Most of our modern institutions, both governmental and private, have adopted the authoritarian model, so that the daily lives of those who work for a living are spent under authority, not in democratic settings. Gradually, democracy has ceased to exist in practice, and we have become accustomed to taking orders, not giving them. These fundamental changes in American society have crept up on us insidiously and invisibly.

In terms of efficiency and power, economic government is far advanced over public government. Eco-

nomic government is based on the latest forms of
organization, technology, and control of communication. Its power derives not from the use of force, as is
the case with public governments, but from its immense wealth, its control over the economic opportunities and security of individuals, and its ability to
engage in economic planning and decision-making
that is no longer undertaken by public government.
Economic government is the dominant partner, public
government the subordinate, in the totality of government that affects our daily lives. Whether the Republicans or Democrats win, economic government
dictates the most important choices and removes these
issues from the political sphere, thus escaping the influence of voters.

But, it will be said, there is no such thing as economic government. Instead, we are observing the operation of the "free market." But is this "market" really
"free"? Coercion marks the employer-employee relationship at every point. For most employees, pay and
working conditions are neither negotiable nor a matter
of free choice. It is "take it or leave it." And few are in
a position to leave it—not when a job is a necessity for
survival. In a true free market, both the buyer and
seller of work or services are free to bargain for the
best possible terms. When that freedom is replaced by
coercion, when one party is dependent upon the other
for survival, there is no longer a free market, and at

precisely that point the actions of the party with a monopoly of economic power *become governmental.*

Through its control of jobs and our livelihood, economic government is responsible for far more coercion in our daily lives than public government. Today, more and more people work under terms of employment they are forced to accept rather than under terms they would demand if bargaining as equals. Employers have forced more and more employees to accept less job security, temporary rather than regular employment, lower pay and benefits than the prosperity of the country would seem to justify, and a steady slide from comfortable middle-class status to the chaos of chronic economic anxiety.

The two most pressing sources of voter discontent, the economic squeeze on the middle-class worker and the social decay and conflict associated with poverty, stem from the decision by economic government to coerce employees into accepting ever-harsher terms while maintaining a permanent class of surplus unemployed persons. Those who are employed even in "good" jobs are forced to work harder and harder, often at the expense of family relationships, while those employed in lower-tier jobs are paid less than a living wage, and those millions for whom no jobs exist are exiled in an underclass. Moral decay, crime, violence, and family breakup are the inevitable consequences of such a social arrangement.

By its treatment of workers, high or low, as disposable machine parts, economic government undermines human values and the ability of individuals to support those values. By its insistence on a steep pyramid of managers and the managed, economic government creates a society shaped not like a democracy but like a corporate hierarchy, with extreme and all-pervasive inequality between the few at the top and the many at the bottom. By its determination to profit at the expense of damaging the less powerful, economic government creates and embraces the conflicts it then promises to solve.

A free market produces results that favor the health of society as a whole, because an essential balance is maintained. But in a coercive market, the balance is destroyed, the earning power of work and the standard of living of workers declines, and society as a whole is devastated while those with economic power gain an ever more unbalanced share of the nation's wealth. Those who preach the virtues of the free market should be the first to recognize that a coercive market is as certain to be destructive as a genuine free market is presumed to be healthy. When the value of labor is forced downward, society ultimately pays the cost of the massive human damage that results. The employer saves on the cost of labor, but imposes a far greater and more lasting cost on individuals and society.

As abundance dries up and only a shrinking waterhole remains, we all turn on each other. Human nature does not fare well under conditions of extreme scarcity. We have plenty of cause to be angry at each others' behavior—to seek punishment and revenge. But the increasingly desperate conditions that bring on this intolerable behavior need not themselves be tolerated. This prolonged dry season is not natural or inevitable. If we could call Adam Smith as an expert witness, he would surely testify that an unfree market destroys the "wealth of nations."

Power of such magnitude that it can change the structure of an entire society must either be based on a truly free market or be deemed governmental—there is no in-between. It does not matter whether a government was elected or simply came into being through the separate actions of individuals and companies. It is the exercise of the power, not its origin, that matters. The System has made a governmental choice, with immense, nationwide consequences: to devalue labor. For most of our history we valued work highly enough so that ordinary Americans could enjoy both security and a rising standard of living. Now a different choice has been made. This new choice structures an entire society in the image of a corporation that has use for people only when they are of economic value. We are now paying the enormous costs of that choice.

Thus we are brought to the second great question

that confronts us: What would constitute an adequate remedy for our present condition? Once we see that the System has failed us, and that we cannot survive its growing inability to meet human needs, the course of action is clear. We must reject the tyranny of economics and revise our economy so that it restores the human habitat, obeys the laws of nature, and offers a secure place to all members of society.

As society suffers ever greater impoverishment and conflict, we would expect, in a democracy, that the people would unite in opposing the System. What prevents us from acting to save ourselves? The System has developed an extraordinary method of maintaining its rule: a map of reality that traps us in our present predicament. Unlike rule by force, rule by control of reality goes undetected and therefore unchallenged. Instead, we accept our decline as due to natural forces beyond our control, and we fight with each other about the best response to the inevitable.

It is time for a restoration of vision. What we need beyond anything else is a new map of reality. Only by seeing the System can we see beyond it. If we can attain a viewpoint outside the System, we will be able to see many choices other than remaining under the domination of a System that promises only worse to come. We can take back our powers. We can regain our citizenship. We can place constitutional limits on the System's use of power. We can find new uses for our energies and new sources of wealth in work that directly nurtures the human economy rather than just the organized economy. We can be more intelligent than the Invisible System, so that we can compel it to serve us better or be replaced. We can reverse the System's downward spiral of violence and repression. We can see beyond the System to a more hopeful vision of abundance and freedom in a society devoted to the needs of nature and human beings. We can fulfill the unfulfilled promise of America.

2

THE INVISIBLE GOVERNMENT

The invisible government hides behind two myths: the myth of the "free market," and the myth of "big government." In fact, the most important changes in America have been the disappearance of the free market and the ineffectuality of public government. Yet public government is all that we see and hear about. We are not told that the growth of public government was a response—a secondary phenomenon. The primary trend has been the growth of private, corporate government. Public government has been repeatedly called upon to protect individuals and society from harm caused by private government, including the Depression of the 1930s. As private corporations and their operations became national and international in scope, state and local governments proved unable to regulate activities beyond their borders.

Private economic government is a far more important factor in the lives of individuals than public government. Private government controls people by controlling their ability to make a living. In order to get a job, have a career, escape the abyss of being rejected or discarded, people will accept the dictates of corporate and institutional employers, even when these dictates go far beyond anything that public government could constitutionally impose. Employers can and do demand a degree of subservience and conformity that public government could never require. Economic punishment is a more effective weapon than the punishment inflicted by law. Dismissal can be a more efficient means of destroying people than the death penalty. Public government is limited in what it can do to individuals by the provisions of the Constitution; private government is subject to no such limitations.

Prior to World War II, the presence of private economic power was a major issue in American life. William Jennings Bryan's populism, Theodore Roosevelt's trustbusting, Woodrow Wilson's New Freedom, and Franklin D. Roosevelt's New Deal were all responses to private economic power. Public government, labor unions, and small business were all viewed as a counterforce. Then, after World War II, the whole subject of private government vanished from public discourse. During the past forty years, private power grew far beyond the size that had previously caused such concern, but it remained out of sight. Voters for-

got why public government existed and saw it, rather
than private government, as the cause of problems fac-
ing the individual. We refused to recognize that a basic
change had taken place in American society—that access to wealth and position had come under tight control, and that the manager, rather than the public
official, held primary authority over people's lives.
Charles Lindblom writes:

> It has been a curious feature of democratic
> thought that it has not faced up to the private
> corporation as a peculiar organization in an
> ostensible democracy. Enormously large,
> rich in resources, the big corporations, we
> have seen, command more resources than
> do most government units. They can also,
> over a broad range, insist that government
> meet their demands, even if these demands
> run counter to those of citizens expressed
> through their polyarchal controls. Moreover,
> they do not disqualify themselves from play-
> ing the partisan role of a citizen—for the cor-
> poration is legally a person. And they
> exercise unusual veto powers. They are on all
> these counts disproportionately powerful,
> we have seen. The large private corporation
> fits oddly into democratic theory and vision.
> Indeed, it does not fit.[1]

The rise and transformation of the corporation parallels the public history of America since the Constitution was adopted. The earliest corporate forms appeared to pose no challenge to the newly established republic. The corporate form was narrowly restricted. But it was not long before the expansive drive of the corporation began to overcome first one limitation and then others.

Americans have become so inured to the corporation's major role in our economic life that we must struggle to remember that this was not always so. The history of how the economy became so highly organized is a narrative both forgotten and repressed, largely omitted from our textbooks and history courses. One place where that history can be found is in a classic opinion by Supreme Court Justice Louis D. Brandeis, written in 1933.[2]

According to Justice Brandeis, Americans in the nineteenth century were long reluctant to grant corporate privileges for doing business, although the efficiency of the corporate form was fully recognized. Corporate privileges were denied "because of fear. Fear of encroachment upon the liberties and opportunities of the individual. Fear of the subjection of labor to capital. Fear of monopoly." Even when privileges were granted, "severe restrictions upon the size and upon the scope of corporate activity" were retained as "an expression of the desire for equality of opportunity."

"The powers which the corporation might exercise in carrying out its purposes were sparingly conferred and strictly construed." Gradually, however, state governments yielded to overwhelming pressure and removed limitations upon the size and activities of business corporations. In consequence, huge concerns developed "in which the lives of tens or hundreds of thousands of employees, and the property of tens or hundreds of thousands of investors are subjected, through the corporate mechanism, to the control of a few men." What evolved, according to Brandeis, was a corporate system comparable to the feudal system, committing American society "to the rule of a plutocracy." As the greater part of the nation's industrial wealth passed from individual possession into the hands of corporations controlled by a few hundred persons, there was a "negation of industrial democracy," a "marked concentration and greater disparity of incomes." "Such," said Justice Brandeis, "is the Frankenstein monster which states have created by their corporation laws."

Justice Brandeis concluded his history by accusing the giant corporation of having played a key role in bringing on the Great Depression and impoverishing the nation:

There is a widespread belief that the existing unemployment is the result, in large part, of the gross inequality in the distribution of

wealth and income which giant corporations
have fostered; that by the control which the
few have exerted through giant corporations,
individual initiative and effort are being par-
alyzed, creative power impaired, and human
happiness lessened; that the true prosperity
of our past came not from big business, but
through the courage, the energy, and the re-
sourcefulness of small men; that only by re-
leasing from corporate control the faculties
of the unknown many, only by reopening to
them the opportunities for leadership, can
confidence in our future be restored and the
existing misery be overcome; and that only
through participation by the many in the responsibilities and determinations of business, can Americans secure the moral and
intellectual development which is essential
to the maintenance of liberty.[3]

In the sixty years since Justice Brandeis wrote,
the trends he described have continued. Every form of
legal control over the corporation has failed. Control
by the stockholders—the supposed owners of corporations—was lost to management. Ownership was thus
separated from control, with management free to pursue its own course without genuine supervision by the
"owners." The device of nonvoting stock was utilized to

keep most stockholders powerless while a small inside group—or sometimes just a single individual—reserved voting rights for themselves. A second kind of legal control—the antitrust laws—also failed. Passed by Congress at the end of the nineteenth century to prevent monopolies, anticompetitive mergers and other restraints of trade, the antitrust laws have remained on the books but have simply not been enforced. The Department of Justice under both Republican and Democratic administrations has looked the other way while ever more gigantic mergers have taken place, and the courts have "interpreted" the antitrust laws to permit many of the practices which the authors of the laws sought to prevent.

A third attempted legal limit on corporate power was regulatory legislation, some dating back to the Progressive Era, some a product of the New Deal. Today, much of this regulation has been repealed or rejected. Another restraint on corporate power, the labor union, has been so weakened that it no longer serves as the counterforce it was expected to be during the New Deal. As corporate operations have become international in scope, even sovereign states have been unable to exert effective control over multinationals, which in some cases are virtually sovereign states themselves. Today, the Fortune 500 dominate American life. By the year 2010, will it be the Fortune 50 or the Fortune 5?

So long as corporations, no matter what their size,

are seen as remaining in the area of business, it is possible to imagine that the other areas of society continue to function as before. But if corporations begin to exercise functions that are governmental, then a structural change takes place that alters the premise of constitutional government.

In 1993, Lauren Allen was a sales associate in the sporting goods department of the new Wal-Mart in Johnstown, New York. The mother of a two-year-old son and a four-year-old daughter, she had separated from her husband. Several months after starting work, she began dating Samuel Johnson, another sales associate in the same department who was single at the time, seeing him after work for bowling or a meal, often in the company of other coworkers. They fell in love. Then Wal-Mart discovered their relationship. The corporation's handbook for employees states: "Wal-Mart strongly believes in and supports the 'family unit.' A dating relationship between a married associate and another associate, other than his or her own spouse, is not consistent with this belief and is prohibited." Ms. Allen was summoned to the store manager's office and asked if she was dating Mr. Johnson. When she acknowledged the relationship, both were dismissed from their jobs. Neither was able to obtain comparable employment elsewhere. Ms. Allen found work folding hospital sheets and towels at a dry cleaner; Mr. Johnson worked as a stock clerk in a lumberyard. The

young couple, aged twenty-three and twenty, live together. "I don't think it was right, what they did," Ms.
Allen said. "I felt it was my personal life. It wasn't interfering with my job. . . . I didn't think it was right that
they could dictate to me in that way."[4]

The rules that corporations make and enforce are
not adopted democratically, nor are they enforced with
the fairness required by due process of law. The workplace is authoritarian and hierarchical. It is ruled from
the top down. Because the workplace is an economic
necessity for most Americans, they have little choice
but to submit to its discipline. But this creates a major
conflict with democracy. When corporations make and
enforce their own laws, they supersede the democratic
process and threaten the core values of representative
government.

We are told that democracy is the best form of
government, and we have fought wars and spent trillions of dollars in a seemingly successful effort to preserve democracy here and abroad. Yet the democratic
model is losing out to the authoritarian model in our
daily lives here at home. Following the corporate lead,
virtually all of our institutions, from schools and col-
leges to Little League, are based on the top-down
model. If we spend most of our time working under
authority, how can we say we are a democratic society? When and where do we practice democracy?

No matter how much governmental power corporations exercise over their employees, corporations are exempt from the Bill of Rights. They do not have to allow their employees freedom of speech, or due process of law, except where statutes explicitly so require. The reason for this exemption is that the Bill of Rights applies only to actions by the government and its agencies, and no matter how "governmental" the actions of corporations may in fact be, the courts continue to treat corporations as if they were truly private when it comes to the Bill of Rights. Corporations are glad to accept their exempt status, since rights are obstacles to economic efficiency, and corporations do not welcome legislation that requires them to observe employees' rights.

The result of this corporate exemption from the Bill of Rights is that employees lose many of their rights as citizens when inside the workplace. Moreover, workplace rules may often extend to nonworkplace times and places, so that the employee's space for full citizenship can shrink even further. An employee who exercises his or her free speech rights outside the workplace is not protected against adverse employer reaction, even though this speech is protected by the Bill of Rights against governmental retaliation. This makes the Bill of Rights a hollow guarantee for many employees, since they may risk jobs or promotions by exercising their full rights as citizens. And the real impact of this diminution of citizenship is felt not only by

the comparatively few employees who get fired for exercising their rights but by the great mass of employees
who are afraid to risk their employers' disapproval.
These employees allow their economic dependency to
become docility; they are afraid to be free. The corporations which dominate these employees have successfully leveraged economic power into political power
that undercuts the Constitution.

As the size and power of business enterprises increased, this great change caused the size and nature
of government to increase in response. So-called big
government is thus a creation of corporate power, not
its antithesis. The Constitution set up a national government of carefully limited and specifically enumer-
ated powers, a government that would not and could
not interfere with a large zone of economic and personal freedom for individuals. But toward the end of
the nineteenth century the growth of corporations created problems which the government was soon called
upon to solve. Small businesses and farmers were
squeezed or forced out of business. Consumers found
themselves confronting prices fixed by monopolies.
Workers experienced disadvantage in bargaining with
their corporate employers. Workers and consumers
found that corporations had little concern for their
health and safety. The economy was subjected to wild
swings from boom to bust, causing periods of frightening insecurity, mass unemployment, and misery. In-

creasingly, the people turned to government for help in dealing with these and other problems which even the most competent of individuals, farmers, and small businesses could not cope with by themselves.

In order to fulfill its new role government needed to expand its constitutional powers. Under the Constitution, amendment would have been the appropriate method of change. Instead, a different process of constitutional change evolved. The U.S. Supreme Court gave new and broader "interpretations" to the words of the Constitution. Thus a constitutional revolution occurred not through the process of amendment envisioned by the framers, but with the consent of the American people.[5] This process of judicial reinterpretation reached its height during the New Deal. Armed with an expanded charter, government undertook to regulate parts of the economy and perform the tasks made necessary by the corporate system but which corporations themselves were unable or unwilling to perform, such as rescuing the nation from downswings in the business cycle. Government was supposed to exercise its expanded powers in a way that was fair to all the factions and interests in society, including labor, farmers, and small business, as well as the corporate sector. But this position of neutrality did not survive the end of World War II. After the war, government became more of a partner to the corporate sector than a neutral. More and more of its help went to the corporate sector, less and less to individuals or the economically weak. The ironic result was that government's expanded constitutional powers, meant to curb and offset corporate power, were now *added* to corporate power.

Today, we have forgotten the reason for the growth of government, because we deny and repress the fact of corporate governmental power. Today's rhetorical attacks on "big government" for interfering with business have largely succeeded in obscuring the fact that it is big business, not big government, that primarily regulates the lives of ordinary Americans. Until "big government" intervened, corporations were free to exploit child labor. Until "big government" protected workers' bargaining, corporations could pay less than a living wage. Until "big government" provided unemployment compensation and Social Security benefits, the worker cast off by a corporate employer had nowhere to turn. When corporate management of the economy resulted in the loss of jobs by millions of willing workers during the Great Depression, it was "big government" that came to the rescue.

The use of the term "welfare state" is a way of disguising the fact that the real issue is economic insecurity and poverty, attributable to the narrowing of economic opportunity and the loss of economic independence that American workers have experienced as a result of corporate dominance of the labor market.

The "welfare state" was needed because of corporate-caused deprivation. On their own, individuals below the top cannot command enough for their only asset—their labor—to pay for their lifetime needs, including education, security, and the support of families.

Similar in principle is the role of government in undertaking to support public services and public goods, which individuals cannot produce on their own and for which corporations do not take responsibility—from national defense and police to national parks, airports, highways, and schools. Schools, for example, benefit individuals but also render an essential service to corporations by providing an educated workforce. Highways are another service to economic activity as well as to the public.

Once government had been expanded to enable it to regulate, to offer positive assistance, and to extend its influence into the economic life of the nation, then a step unforeseen by the New Deal thinkers occurred: All of these new powers were redirected to favor corporate power and disfavor labor, small farmers and businesses, and the individual. Regulatory agencies created to restrain corporate power were filled with appointees friendly to big business. The social programs intended to help the needy were steadily cut back and hedged with restrictions while aid to corporations became more openhanded. Trillions were spent on the cold war defense buildup; much of this money went to enrich giant corporate defense contractors such as Boeing, General Dynamics, and General Electric. The tax laws became an elaborate source of favors and giveaways as, under the rubric of "tax expenditures" and "tax incentives," tax breaks and tax subsidies for big business were written into the Internal Revenue code. Oil leases, timber sales, and other subsidized distributions of public resources flowed to corporations where once (as under the Homestead Act) public lands had been a source of support for individuals.

A crucial illustration of how governmental powers intended to strengthen democracy were transformed into vital supports for corporate power is the story of how radio and television licenses were distributed. All of the radio and television channels are publicly owned and remain so. The stations and networks that utilize these channels are licensees of the federal government. Originally it was intended that broadcast licenses be allocated by the Federal Communications Commission to a broad variety of community groups and interests representative of American pluralism and obligated to use their broadcasting privileges to further "the public interest." What has happened instead is that corporate giants, especially those already in control of other forms of mass communication such as newspapers, gathered the lion's share of the licenses, often controlling multiple stations. In addition, the major networks and stations have been given over exclusively to commercial use, so that they are dominated by large corporate advertisers. Despite the fact that these broadcast licenses are worth many millions of dollars to the licensees, the licensees neither share their profits with the public (as owners) nor perform any but the most token public services. As great as is this giveaway of wealth, the giveaway of power is even more significant. It means that corporate America completely dominates the *public* airways, and nothing that is disapproved of by corporate America is likely to be heard by the public.

It is in the area of control of knowledge and ideas that the merger of governmental and corporate power reaches its apex. At the same time that government began to change from a neutral protector of the public interest under the New Deal to a partner of corporate America, an elaborate program was instituted to cleanse government of anyone who still believed in the New Deal vision. This was the so-called loyalty program—so called because it purported to be aimed at Communists, subversives, and persons disloyal to the United States, but in fact was aimed at those in government who still held the New Deal values and goals. Beginning in the late 1940s, and continuing to the present day, persons wishing to work for the government, whether nominated to the Supreme Court or offered a student summer internship at the Department of Justice, or anything in between, have been subjected to "background checks" by the FBI or other investigative agencies, designed to elicit personal and political information ranging from sexual orthodoxy to political conformity as the test of eligibility for public office or appointment. Friends and former friends and associates are interrogated to make sure that no independent thinker is allowed to hold a government job. All dissenting ideas are thus kept entirely outside of government counsels—including ideas about the proper relationship of government to corporate America. Even though the cold war is over and the red scare is a thing of the past, these police checks of political and personal behavior continue in full force.

As government became more clearly allied with business, the legal system lost whatever neutrality it possessed and became a pliable tool of power. The wealth that government distributes and the advantages that government confers must be based upon some form of legal authorization. But when law is employed to justify this process, the ideal of "equal justice under law" disappears and respect for the law is lost. While an unemployed worker receives less than enough compensation to live on, a rancher obtains government-subsidized grazing privileges of great value, a lumber company gets to use the national forests for very substantial profit, and the recipient of a defense contract obtains a privilege worth millions of dollars. Most legally authorized favors and advantages are the result of successful lobbying or other uses of power and influence. Groups like the poor, which lack power and influence, end up with the smallest share of government bounty. Obtaining government wealth thus becomes an insiders' game. Those on the outside are the losers.

The law is full of justifications of the disparate treatment accorded the many classes of citizens and businesses. But these explanations cannot hide favors based upon power and influence. The neutrality, fairness, and dignity of law is destroyed by its involvement in this game of government favors. Lawlessness becomes difficult to distinguish from the advantageous use of law. The person who acquires wealth with the help of a gun may see himself as no different from the person who acquires wealth with the help of a tax break or favorable agency ruling, except that the latter is not subject to punishment and usually walks off with a far greater gain. Why should the dispossessed respect the authority of law? The outsider's crime may seem morally no different from the insider's coup.

The increasing merger of governmental and corporate interests has been further solidified by the emergence of a trained group of managers who moved easily and interchangeably from the corporate to the public sector and back again. The existence of this managerial elite allows both sectors to make important decisions on the basis of shared knowledge and shared assumptions without any conspiracy or overt coordination. The most basic choices can be taken out of the hands of the people and made in undemocratic fashion without any visible signs of how this is accomplished. Even members of the elite do not necessarily recognize the coordinated decision-making process of which they are a part.

The managerial elite is formed on the basis of shared knowledge and assumptions. The shared knowledge is acquired in school, college, professional school, and later on at work. Like other significant features of the System, this shared knowledge has no name, is never directly taught, is not written down, and prefers invisibility. The starting point of the elite's shared knowledge is that every member of the elite discovered the road to success, which the vast majority never find. For example, the road to success involves passing tests, from elementary school to graduate or professional school, and then in the lower rungs of the public or corporate bureaucratic ladder. The many years of test-passing give rise to a knowledge of what is required to satisfy those who create and administer the tests, and what will bring about rejection. Our present managers may be the most thoroughly tested group of individuals who ever lived on the planet. What are they tested for? The answer is: skills that advance the interests of the System. But these skills are not necessarily the same as the substantive skills of the doctor, the auto worker, the farmer. The people who run our society may not be the best at the usual categories of human achievement, but they are the best at rising to the top of the System.

The elite are set apart from those who lack all power in the workplace and are required to do work that is an alienating experience because of repetition, hazardousness, oppressive supervision, lack of respect, or other bad conditions. The elite have been able to make their jobs personally rewarding and gratifying, so that they find pleasure in work as well as in monetary compensation. The elite generally enjoy job security, high esteem, opportunities for self-expression, and the ability to pass their status along to their children. Their job gives them an income in intangibles that may be worth many times their monetary pay. Their greatest reward may be a sense of power. They possess influence. They can make things happen. They can get other people jobs and rewards. If they are high enough, they can influence the nation's thinking. They are "in the loop," "inside the Beltway," or otherwise closely connected to the mind of the System.

The elite do not know what the world is like for the nonelite, even if they come from a nonelite background. They do not know the causes of nonsuccess. The elite do not experience the consequences of the policies they set and the decisions they make. The elite do not understand unfairness, for life has been more than fair to them. They do not see how a deserving person can fail, except by his or her own weakness. To the elite, the world looks rational and orderly. To those at the bottom, the world looks unfair, random, cruel, and chaotic.

The elite live in a different country than the rest of Americans. It is not possible to understand the System and its actions without understanding this fact. The elite sees its own ascendancy as just, and cannot understand the anger below. Yet the rules for success used by the elite are often very different from the rules observed by ordinary people. This leads the elite to believe that those below "cannot be told" the real reasons for decisions that are made. The question becomes what should the people be told, not what are the facts. The perplexity of the voter who tries first one party and then the other, winding up always with the same elite, shows how democracy has given way to the rule of the System's managers.

Shared knowledge leads to shared assumptions, which are even more crucial than knowledge in making it possible for the elite managers to work together without "conspiracy." These invisible shared assumptions are the real Constitution, the real fundamental law, which guides the System:

First. Impersonal economic "forces" produce better decisions and choices than can be made by even the most thoughtful individuals or groups attempting to weigh the competing interests of society. Often called "market forces," they are venerated and deferred to even when the "market" is impaired, dominated, or nonexistent.

Second. "Economic growth" is a measure of the well-being of the society as a whole. Such growth benefits all the elements and individuals in society. There is no need for "Gross Domestic Product" to be offset by a compilation of "Gross Domestic Cost." "Growth" can be counted on to create new jobs and wider individual opportunity.

Third. All of the important social values affected by the economic system are measurable and quantifiable. Intangible or "soft" interests such as trust, loyalty, community, natural beauty, or sacredness are separate from the economic process and may be "willed" by individuals of strong enough character and a high enough sense of personal responsibility. For example, care of children is a matter of "will," not economics.

Fourth. The treatment of people in their role as employees does not affect the rest of their lives. For example, an authoritarian workplace does not diminish or impair a worker's ability to practice democracy outside the workplace. Summary layoffs and terminations after years of service do not affect workers' capacity for loyalty, or for commitment to loved ones. Coercion on the job does not lead to an increase of coercive behavior off the job.

Fifth. The market may be counted on to supply human and social needs even though a massive and unrelenting effort is made to influence consumer preferences, no opposing view of needs is allowed to reach the public by way of the media, and the consumer has received no information about society's need for balance, diversity, or long-term investment. No alternative method of planning for the future is required.

Sixth. People are rational actors whose behavior can be motivated, controlled, channeled, and deterred by threats and promises of economic gain and loss, by repression and punishment, by constant competition against others, and by orders issued by those in superior positions. Economic self-interest is expected to dominate human behavior, but people can be expected to forgo self-interest in their personal lives in favor of heightened responsibility to others and to "the community."

Seventh. The ultimate product of society is the best possible System, not the best possible human beings.

Given these shared assumptions, the corporate elite and the governmental elite together make the most important decisions affecting society, often overriding what voters choose at the polls. What remains for presidential candidates to debate or for Congress to vote on is most often trivial and irrele-

vant, incapable of overturning the more basic decisions that are made in nondemocratic fashion. It is as
if the Constitution had been amended to include the
following provision:

MANAGERIAL REVIEW

Policies and choices made by voters as part
of the electoral process shall be subject to
review by a Board of Managers representing
the governmental and corporate sectors. The
Board may, in its absolute discretion, con-
firm or reverse decisions by the electorate or
substitute other policies for those chosen by
the electorate.

It is important to dismiss the stereotypes of the
past. This is not the corporate trust, monopoly, or oli-
gopoly of the past. It is not a conspiracy; there are no
old-time capitalists in shiny top hats hatching plots.
The decisions of today are made in far more sophisti-
cated fashion by a consensus that does not require
conscious choice by separate executives or companies,
but merely acquiescence in underlying assumptions,
and concerted action based on those assumptions. It is
often said that "big government" has too much power,
that "big government" is too intrusive, that "big government" interferes with the everyday lives and opportunities of individuals. But the power of combined

economic government and public government is vastly greater than this, and those who participate in its exercise are not necessarily conscious of the impact of their decisions on ordinary people's lives.

The decision that most directly affects the lives of ordinary Americans concerns the structure of work and the workforce. The workforce has been reshaped into an ever steeper pyramid, with fewer and fewer people enjoying a greater and greater share of wealth and privilege at the top; more and more workers thrown into a "lower tier" of reduced pay, benefits, and security; and a permanent surplus of unemployed at the bottom ready to take any job that becomes available and thus making the working population easily replaceable and therefore unable to demand higher wages and better terms and conditions. It is this decision that is destroying the middle class, driving more and more people into desperation and poverty, separating the population into antagonistic classes of extreme wealth and powerless subservience, and creating the dissatisfaction that drives the demand for change.

Everyone's life has been changed by this decision. Only forty years ago the shape of the workforce was very different, with a broad and affluent middle class as the most important stabilizing feature of American life. Now, workers who "play by the rules" are steadily losing ground, and frustration, fear, and anger has stolen their dreams. Opportunity is greatly diminished by this decision, security is lost, antagonism is engendered, community is destroyed. And yet Americans have passively accepted this prime example of unwanted social change, believing it to be not a decision at all, but the result of impersonal economic forces that no one can or should control.

What this explanation overlooks is that the present structure of the workforce is not the result of competition and the free play of economic forces, but the product of the absence of competition. So long as corporate power was offset by strong labor unions and by a government representing all classes in society, an upwardly mobile workforce existed. Only when corporate power reached the point of ability to control the workforce without interference by unions, government, or competition from other corporations for workers, did the situation change. The change took place because of the growth of uncontested power. Global competition does not dictate the extreme inequality of our hierarchical workforce. As is well known, the other industrial countries with which we compete, such as Japan and Germany, have far less disparity between the pay of top executives and workers. Sharing the pie more equally among executives and workers would not diminish the profitability of the enterprise as a whole.

The way voter choice can be reversed by the

managerial elite is illustrated by the raising of interest rates in 1994 despite the negative effects of this action on employment. In the 1992 presidential campaign, Bill Clinton promised a pro-employment policy that would reduce joblessness, raise the minimum wage, favor "good jobs" (not part-time or dead-end employment), and provide extensive job training and retraining. The minimum wage increase was not enacted; the budget failed to include significant funds for training and job stimulus, and by 1994 the Clinton administration had quietly accepted the Federal Reserve Board's program of raising interest rates at the expense of employment. What the people voted for at the polls was reversed by the invisible managerial structure. Reporter Thomas L. Friedman of the *New York Times* wrote:

> But what is implicit in such moves [raising interest rates] is the following assumption: that America has decided that in the tradeoff between job growth and inflation growth, between putting people back to work and putting up prices a little, jobs are less important. Higher mortgage rates and more unemployment be damned. But this has left a lot of people asking: "Who decided that?" "Was there a vote I missed?" "Why should I be held hostage by the bond market?"[6]

A second major decision that affects the lives of ordinary Americans is how we will spend our money —on toys for children or schools for children, on entertainment or public libraries, on expensive automobiles or preserving natural beauty. In a free economy, this is a choice that is supposed to be made by the people. When we find ourselves asking, as we now do, "What has happened to the money?"—for schools, for universities, for child care, for parks, for other elements of any good society—we are revealing that we have lost this sovereign power of choice. If we had consciously made a decision not to spend our resources on such goods as education, there would be no mystery, even if we had made an unwise choice. The mystery arises when we cannot find the money for the goods we say we want.

In his classic work *The Affluent Society* (1958), John Kenneth Galbraith made the important observation that our economy showed an increasing pattern of affluence in the private sector combined with impoverishment of the public sector. Galbraith described the "public poverty" of urban decay, school overcrowding, insufficient public transportation, air and water pollution, shortages of parks and playgrounds, and a commercially blighted countryside. He pointed out that privately produced wealth was in startling contrast to the impoverishment of publicly rendered goods and services, and that "our wealth in privately produced goods is, to a marked degree, *the cause of crisis in the supply of public services*"[7] (emphasis added).

This observation by Galbraith more than thirty-five years ago has proven to be a dire prophesy: In the ensuing decades, we have seen more and more "public poverty," which has caused ever deeper cutbacks in spending for all the public needs of society except for police, prisons, and the military—the instrumentalities of repression. This public impoverishment is caused by giving an almost absolute priority to "private" economic growth. Galbraith points out, for example, that advertising operates exclusively on behalf of privately produced goods. "The engines of mass communication, in their highest state of development, assail the eyes and ears of the community on behalf of more beer but not of more schools. Even in the conventional wisdom it will scarcely be contended that this leads to an equal choice between the two."[8] And Galbraith offers several other substantial reasons why public goods are at a severe disadvantage in competing with private growth. Today's "mystery" of no money for public services turns out to be no mystery at all. The missing money is to be found in the "private sector."

What Galbraith could not imagine in 1958 was how far the process of neglecting public services would go, and the zeal with which "deficit reduction" (i.e., still further cuts in public expenditures) would be pursued by leaders of both political parties. Nor could he have anticipated the national denial that public services are in many cases essential to the health of society, whereas the goods and services of the private sector may be unnecessary luxuries.

Linda Davidoff writes in the *New York Times:*

New York City seems determined to squeeze its Parks Department dry. In 1986 the department had 4,951 full-time employees—meager by the standards of other cities—to seed, mow, clean, prune, paint and repair 26,000 acres of ballfields, paths, woodlands, beaches, meadows, and flower gardens. By 1995, if Mayor Rudolph W. Giuliani's budget is adopted, the full-time staff will have fallen to 2,563. . . .[9]

Across the nation, parks, both urban and wilderness, are suffering a comparable tragic neglect. And this neglect lessens everyone's enjoyment and leads more and more people to feel a sense of claustrophobia that there is no longer beauty, or wildness, or sanctuary to be found.

Thus the two great decisions that make the most difference to ordinary Americans were not made by "big government" or by the voters but by unelected managers who are well isolated against the effects of their own decisions. Why do we passively accept this

situation when we find the results so painful and un-
satisfactory? The answer is that we have been led to
believe that these decisions are being made not by
managers but by "the free market." Despite overwhelming evidence that the free market is a myth, it is universally spoken of as if it were the central truth about
our economy. It is not.

The great irony of the free-market myth is that it is
perpetuated by the very same corporations which have
done everything possible to eliminate the free market.
From the very beginning, the corporation has had one
primary goal—control. The purpose of large-size, massive accumulations of capital and the organization of
production by many workers is usually given as "efficiency"—and the large corporation has indeed proved
more efficient at many tasks than individuals or small
firms. Thus it is difficult to imagine anything smaller
than a large corporation running a steel mill or producing automobiles or operating an airline. "The efficiency
of large scale" is an axiom of economics. But what un-
derlies efficiency is *control*. The larger the corporation,
the better it can control the entire process of acquiring
raw materials, manufacturing a product, and distribut-
ing and marketing the product. The efficiency of Henry
Ford's assembly line lay in its control of the activities of
thousands of workers, suppliers, and distributors.
Hence from the very beginning the effect of the large
corporation was to undermine those two cherished

eighteenth-century institutions which lay at the foundation of America—the free market and democracy.

Corporations wanted a market, but not a free market. They wanted the power to fix the terms and conditions of employment on a take-it-or-leave-it basis and to fix the cost of materials and the price of finished products in the same way. Therefore, the natural tendency of the corporate system was toward *combination* and *concentration*. Corporations combined *vertically* to control each step of the production process, from acquiring raw materials to consumer sales. Independent suppliers or distributors might retain a measure of freedom to bargain, but where they became subsidiaries of the manufacturer that freedom gave way to control. Corporations also combined *horizontally* to control every area of the country; for example, having identical retail outlets from Maine to Florida and from New York to California. Horizontal combination means that whenever a consumer tries to buy a product, she finds the identical choice, not a range of choices.

The free-market myth denies the success of all of these efforts at merger, combination, concentration, and control. Theodore Lowi writes:

> . . . it would be closer to the truth to propose that at no time in the past century or more was there a period when society in the United

States was anywhere nearly self-regulating
... the administrative component has developed in hand with the technological, the
commercial, and the pluralistic components.
The development was simply taking place in
the private sector. ...

A look inside the larger corporations in
the United States helps specify the elements
of the private administrative component.
Pricing and production decisions have long
been removed from the market by an immense planning, programming, and research apparatus. Undoubtedly many an
American giant had the equivalent of a
Five-Year Plan earlier than did the Soviet
government. ...[10]

The key to both the ability of the System to make
the most important economic decisions by command
and its ability to conceal this fact by using the free-
market myth lies in the System's control of communications, knowledge, and opinion. No challenge to the
free-market myth is heard on television or radio; the
economics profession solidly perpetuates the myth;
and meanwhile the decisions that are actually made
are then pressed on the American people from every
direction. Charles Lindblom describes a "command
economy" as one that embraces the *full range of meth-*

ods of control.... It seeks to control the mind, as far as possible, by *controlling all forms of communication...."* (italics in original).[11] We too live under a system that seeks to control the mind by making invisible what is really happening and covering the truth with myth.

The managerial system has proven immensely successful for business. It is far more efficient, at least in the short run, than the slower democratic model. In theory, managerialism might also provide the best possible government for a high-tech society in the twenty-first century. If top executives produced a healthy and happy society as the bottom line of their endeavors, they might be worth the multimillion-dollar salaries some are now paid. But for a managerial system to succeed, it would have to be subjected to a larger framework of control. The managers would have to be held responsible for serving the best interests of society as a whole. They would have to preserve our basic values of equality, individual rights, and ultimate respect for the people. In contrast, our present managerial system is not controlled by any outside structure. It does not even purport to serve the best interests of society, and it escapes responsibility for the disastrous conditions it creates.

Driven by the goal of economic efficiency, harnessing the forces of competition and human desire, utilizing the latest advances in organization and technology, the managerial system has proved to be a dynamic and expansive competitor to the older forms of constitutional democracy and the free market. The fact that the managerial system is *in competition* with these older forms, rather than simply coexisting with them, has not been adequately recognized. Instead, it has always been tacitly assumed that the managerial system would confine itself to business activities and not threaten the larger contours of democracy, the Constitution, and the free market. This assumption, that management would remain confined within the existing structure of society, has proven false. Instead, management has demonstrated a powerful drive for expansion, leading it to seek and gain control over both government and the free market, until the managerial system has reached a point where it pervasively influences everything else in society. But the very characteristics which give the managerial system its power make it unsuitable for the governance of an entire society. Applied to society as a whole, the strengths of managerialism become weaknesses, and its drive for efficiency becomes a power to destroy.

In its drive for economic efficiency, the managerial system is single-minded: It has but one goal, the maximization of profit. By contrast, a society must have multiple goals, must promote a thriving diversity, must seek a balance among many interests. The single-mindedness of a management seeking purely economic

gain rejects all other social and human needs. For example, the managerial system is highly selective; it
wants only those workers it can utilize with maximum
efficiency, and casts aside other workers who are
deemed surplus. But a society as a whole has to be
inclusive, and it must offer a place to everyone. It cannot reject people because they are inefficient. A managerial system seeks flexibility; it is ready to discard
people the moment they are not needed. On the other
hand, most people require security and stability; human beings are not as adaptable as machine parts and
cannot build lives upon a foundation of perpetual uncertainty. A managerial system is authoritarian and
hierarchical; it does not recognize the values of equality, democratic participation, or organic community.
It treats people as interchangeable machine parts,
whereas a true community regards every individual as
unique. A managerial system has no concern with human needs. It will make and sell whatever brings a
profit, and refuse to make whatever does not bring a
profit, irrespective of what people need to become well-
functioning individuals, families, and communities.

Rights are inefficient. Fair procedures are inefficient. Constitutional limitations are inefficient.
Democratic dialogue is inefficient. Self-government is
inefficient. Nonconformity is inefficient. Dignity is inefficient. The managerial system is impatient with all
of these. If the cheap labor of an authoritarian country

can lower the cost of a product, management prefers that choice to the work of individuals endowed with rights and dignity.

These limitations of a managerial system prevent it from being a sustainable model for an entire society. But they have not prevented it from taking over control of society and its institutions. This is one of the great weaknesses of present-day public philosophy: It assumes, without any basis, that such a takeover will not occur despite the fact that managerialism has amply demonstrated the power to cross any and all boundaries. Instead, corporate wealth and influence have allowed management to conscript government. The state is supposed to prevail over all other forms in society because the state has a monopoly of force, but corporate wealth has been able to prevail over force. Nothing is more crucial to classical economic thought than the separation of government from the business sector, yet the merger of public and private is a fact of life. Economic power can be leveraged to exert political power. Corporate wealth is leveraged to control expression in the media. Corporate power over livelihood becomes control over the private lives of workers. Corporate dominance of entertainment is leveraged to control American culture. Corporate donations to universities becomes control over scholarship and thought.

The managerial system presents virtually every possible contrast with both the conservative and the liberal vision of a pluralistic, self-governing republic. A great intellectual failure of both conservatives and liberals has been their inability or unwillingness to recognize this fundamental conflict. And since the conflict itself is unobserved, neither conservatives nor liberals have proposed any method of resolving or presiding over the conflict, whether by means of structure, philosophy, a return to older traditions, or some new social invention.

The invisibility and denial which obscure the unprecedented power concentrated in economic government also enable it to escape the responsibility that should accompany such power. Today, all of the talk about responsibility is directed at the most powerless people in our society. The powerful call for responsibility by the dispossessed but are silent about the responsibilities of power. They deny that responsibility inescapably accompanies power. A managerial system might serve society well if it were also a responsible system. What is wrong with the present System is not necessarily that it is managerial, but that it is not accountable to the people it serves, and instead serves itself.

The temptations under the present System for those in power, whether in the public or corporate sectors, to serve themselves, particularly in a financial way, are overwhelming. The safeguards are virtually nonexistent. The merger of corporate and governmental sectors brings out and combines the irresponsible side of each. The government becomes infected with the profit motive; the corporate sector uses governmental power without constitutional restraint. Both seek to minimize responsibilities, the corporate sector because responsibilities are costs which reduce profits, the government because responsibilities are bureaucratic failures for which no public official wants to accept blame. Both resort to lies and deception and whenever possible avoid candor with the public. Both seek to shift blame to someone else. Both reflect the absence of a presiding authority; corporations are no longer responsible to their owners, and government is no longer responsible to the sovereign people.

Corporations receive all kinds of public assistance based on the assumption that they will create jobs and benefit the community as a whole. Yet the same corporations cut jobs to increase their profits and devastate communities by moving their operations outside the United States. Their example of nonresponsibility speaks far louder to the poor than their calls for more responsibility by individuals.

Power is an important basis for responsibility, but it is not the only one. In the modern world, responsibility also arises because of expertise. In a technological society like ours, the expert has a special kind of responsibility based on knowledge. When we see a physician or enter a hospital we are placing ourselves in

the care of experts. The patient undergoing surgery
with general anesthesia is in the hands of the expert.
The airline passenger is equally in the care of experts.
So is the client who consults a professional in almost
any area. Thus most experts have been subjected to an
appropriate code of responsibility that is now universally recognized. The expert must, for example, never
place personal gain or convenience above the interests
of those who place their trust in him or her. The expert
must carry out his or her duties with the greatest care
for the safety and well-being of patients or passengers.
The expert has an equal duty to all persons and may
not discriminate unfairly. These canons of professional
responsibility are well known to physicians, attorneys,
teachers, and other established professionals. Managing the economy is also an area of expertise. The workings of the Federal Reserve Board, or the Council of
Economic Advisers, or the Treasury Department are
matters of special knowledge that affect jobs, pay-
checks, and economic opportunities for all Americans.

When power or expertise exists but responsibility
is denied, a gap is created where others are disabled
from acting. By exerting control, the powerful exclude
others from taking necessary actions. By denying responsibility, the powerful create a zone of neglect
where no one can prevent the festering of evils and
decay. It is this zone of neglect that is now spreading
its malign influence across the American landscape,

causing the decay of cities and people. Nothing is more demoralizing than the exercise of control by those who take no responsibility, because it prevents those who are subject to that control from helping themselves.

Our invisible System performs many wonders, but *it is a machine*, a machine harnessing human energy but still a machine. Sixty years ago this metaphor was widely used; New Dealers spoke of "our economic machine." Today we no longer hear this term used to describe our System. Perhaps we have forgotten the metaphor because we have forgotten that a machine requires guidance and control; a machine must have goals set for it from outside; a machine on its own does not care about human beings or the human community.

The System may make itself invisible, but it cannot hide the damage it is causing. All of our efforts to halt that damage have failed because we refuse to see its true cause, limiting ourselves to dealing with symptoms. It is time to replace self-serving myths with a clear view of our economic-political machine. Only then can we command it to serve human needs.

3

ECONOMICS V. SOCIETY

In the 1994 election, voters focused on two great concerns: economic insecurity and social breakdown. Unfortunately, the remedy chosen by newly elected federal and state officials is certain to make things worse. By giving greater freedom to economic forces while stripping protection from individuals and the environment, we accelerate the process of destruction. Economic forces are the cause of both insecurity and social pathology. Nature requires balance. Human society, as a part of nature, also requires balance. The economic must be balanced by the noneconomic. The production of goods and services must not be allowed to destroy the human habitat and the fabric of relationships we call "society." Growth of the economy is beneficial only if this limit is observed. When economic growth disregards this principle, it comes into conflict with the other needs of society. It is this conflict that threatens us now.

Both economic insecurity and social pathology are symptoms of this underlying conflict. In an age of technology, economic forces erode the value of human labor and undermine the security and pay of traditional jobs. Economic forces drive us toward extremes of inequality, in which fewer and fewer "winners" receive an ever-greater proportion of the nation's wealth, while an ever-increasing proportion of "losers," deprived of life's necessities, develop the pathologies which include family breakup and crime. When one discharged postal worker returns with an automatic weapon to wreak suicidal vengeance on anyone and everyone at the workplace, we may call it an individual act. When this same phenomenon is repeated many times in totally unrelated incidents, we must see that larger forces are implicated. The worker subjected to economic death sprays indiscriminate death around him.

There will be no relief from either economic insecurity or human breakdown until we recognize that uncontrolled economic forces create conflict, not well-being. But we cannot see this cause-and-effect relationship so long as we accept the myth that economic growth has only a beneficial side. Our political, business, and intellectual leaders, despite many other differences, all perpetuate this myth. The harmful side of economic growth has been hidden from view, leaving us to blame individuals and groups for insecurity and social decay, thereby dividing society into a warring "us" and "them."

Faith in the absolute goodness of economic growth ignores one crucial piece of evidence. We see with our own eyes that unrestrained economic growth can be destructive to the natural environment and the habitats of plants and animals. Logic suggests that the same process may reach a stage where it adversely affects the human habitat, and that this is manifested in the economic insecurity and social breakdown we are trying to change. We are prevented from making this analysis of our present situation by a rigid ortho-doxy of forced belief. Today, the operation of what are called "free-market forces" is viewed as embodying a perfection similar to the laws of physics and in total contrast to the imperfection of human institutions such as governments. The economy is thought to have no failings so long as humans do not interfere. Faith in free economic forces approaches the status of a secular religion. The absence of restraint, which is frowned upon in the case of individuals and governments, is applauded when applied to the economy. News that government grew is considered bad; news that eco-nomic institutions grew is uniformly hailed as good.

Economic laws are believed to operate with an inevitability that is more powerful than politics or gov-ernments, as if these "laws" derived from a higher source than human beings. Even when they cause

harsh consequences, as in the case of global competition for cheap labor, we are told we must accept these
"laws" as inevitable. We are so grateful to the market
economy for the prosperity of industrial nations and
for America's position in the world that no one wants
to change the presumed basis of America's preemi-
nence. This uncritical trust in economic laws is a recent legacy of the cold war. During most of the
industrial revolution and the rise of capitalism it was
recognized that an industrial economy can inflict great
harm on human beings and on society.

If economic forces are beyond criticism, we are
driven to look elsewhere to explain the spreading ills of
inequality and social decay. Given the assumption that
economic laws represent perfection, ills must be explained as caused by individuals or governments. Both
governments and individuals are then urged to improve themselves by adapting to the imperatives of the
economic system. Government should shrink; individuals should obtain retraining. According to this view, it
is human beings and their institutions that must adapt
to the imperatives of the economic system, not the
economy which must adapt to serve human beings.

It is difficult to challenge a quasi-religious faith.
One of the great obstacles to questioning our economy
is the insistence that there is only one, far worse alternative—some form of communism or socialism. In
fact, socialist economies have proven to be harmful to

human beings in ways remarkably similar to the harms discernible in Western economies; much of what was formerly Eastern Europe is now an ecological disaster area. A true alternative economy would be entirely different from both of these supposed antagonists.

There are powerful reasons to question and challenge our economic religion. Our "economic laws" are human creations, not infallible laws of the natural universe. Even if these laws were once beneficial, they are still subject to reexamination because of profound changes in circumstances and context. The world of 1776, when Adam Smith published his book describing the free market, has been replaced by a centralized and highly organized economy; it is absurd to assume that the Adam Smith economic model still operates in the same way. But the greatest reason for questioning our economic system lies in the spreading disorder and impoverishment that has accompanied recent economic growth. To challenge the religion of economic growth we must understand how what was once good and beneficial has become the major threat to human survival.

In primitive societies, the economy is the equivalent of life itself—all the activities of the community are both economic and noneconomic at the same time. As an economy becomes a highly specialized machine, this unity of economy and life is replaced by a separation into different spheres or realms—economic and noneconomic. Thus the family, which once was both economic and noneconomic, now is part of a realm of personal activities that are located in the noneconomic sphere. The economic machine competes with this personal sphere and represents interests such as organizations that are quite different from the interests of the personal sector. Instead of lending support to the personal sector, the economic machine competes with personal values. Finally, the economic machine becomes so separate from other human interests that it threatens their survival just as it threatens the habitats of the natural environment. In this way a once-beneficial economic system can imperceptibly be transformed into a system that brings increasing damage as well as benefits. Our continuing faith is one more example of a lag in thinking due to unacknowledged social change.

The concept of "growth" may be an unqualified plus when applied to a single organism or unit. A child grows, a tree grows, a bank account grows. But when we are told that the economy of a whole society "grows," we need to remember that an economy is not a single entity but contains a balance of many interests, values, and relationships. Some of these may benefit from growth, others may not. "Growth" may be beneficial to air travel and housing sales, but harmful and destructive to children and families. Evils as well as good things may "grow." Thus "growth" as applied to an economy should be expected to represent harm as well as good. We should apply the perspective gained from the study of ecology to the human ecosystem as it undergoes changes caused by "economic growth." Instead of looking to growth for salvation, we should closely question its impact. How has growth affected workers' pay and security? How does growth affect poverty and unemployment? How has growth affected "public sector" expenditures for schools, parks, and other social needs? What is the impact of growth on that part of the human environment represented by family and other personal activities outside of work?

The harmful side of growth may not be apparent all at once. Instead, it seems likely that growth passes through several distinct stages. Perhaps growth first is widely beneficial, then later adversely affects the natural environment, still later damages the human habitat, and finally destroys the jobs and economic security it was supposed to create. At each stage those who are unaffected fail to take alarm. If growth creates unemployment for some but better jobs for others, those who are still employed will continue to see growth as beneficial. When growth reaches a stage where it causes the earnings of middle-class workers to stagnate or decline, while an ever-smaller elite continues to do better, those on top will find growth beneficial and will continue to describe the economy as "improving." It is hard to recognize that each successive form of damage is part of the same underlying conflict, and that those who ignore damage to the natural environment will one day find their own environment being destroyed in exactly the same way.

Economic growth did not always go unchallenged. Prior to World War II, and during the New Deal, it was widely recognized that, while our ability to *produce* was virtually unlimited, *distribution* remained an unsolved problem. Many New Deal measures were designed to curtail production and to create artificial scarcity simply to maintain prices. We could produce, but we could not find a way to enable people at the lower end of the economic scale to buy. Closely related to this dilemma was the looming question of unemployment and low-quality jobs. Advances in technology meant that fewer workers were needed. This problem of "technological unemployment" had long been apparent. The New Deal put people to work, but only on a short-term, government-financed basis. A further question concerning growth arose from the depletion of natural resources. Although nothing like the post–World War II environmental crisis was visible, the New Deal did seek to curb the kind of economic development that wantonly and wastefully stripped natural resources. Conservation measures became an important New Deal priority.

After World War II most of these concerns about

growth vanished. "Economic growth" became the most universally accepted sign of a society's health and progress. There was as much support for "growth" from one political party as from the other, from labor as from management, from the Left as from the Right. The only disagreement was on how to achieve and maintain a high rate of growth. Decades such as the 1950s were held up as models of prosperity and well-being ascribed to a high rate of growth. Any economic problems were explained by low or "stagnant" growth. Growth, it was repeatedly said, "lifts all boats" like the incoming tide.

In the years following World War II, America was dominated by a coalition made up of both liberals and conservatives who suppressed genuine political debate about priorities and goals in the name of growth. Alan Wolfe writes:

> Since growth was the agreed-upon goal, politics in America would no longer be divided along even minimal class lines, as it was becoming during the New Deal, and would no longer be encumbered by discussions of "issues." Debates would concern means, not ends. Major questions of public policy were simply removed from debate. Growth, in short, presupposed the suppression of fundamental political choice. The purpose of

campaigns and elections was to ratify technical decisions about how expeditiously growth was occurring, not to mandate radical departures in policy.

... neither wing of the growth coalition would seek to mobilize discontent from below, to tap new sources of support among underrepresented groups, or to encourage whatever popular protest existed in society.... "Politics" would come to mean a discussion among interest groups, not an attempt to develop a vision of a better society.... The two wings of the growth coalition deeply needed each other, and while they would engage in political combat in public, they would often arrange harmonious compromises in private.[1]

Wolfe shows that the growth coalition suppressed political debate and choice concerning underlying issues such as discrimination, poverty, unemployment, the distribution of wealth, and public spending. As a result, the possibility that growth was causing greater inequality and social neglect was never considered, even though the nation suffered from stubborn poverty, urban riots, and other signs of underlying trouble. Warnings that we were becoming a racially divided society were also ignored, as was the physical decay of cities. While growth remained sacrosanct, the slow and stealthy advance of impoverishment continued. Every form of growth was added together to produce a highly visible and much-publicized grand total—the Gross Domestic Product. Impoverishment was kept invisible by being *disaggregated*. Each item of impoverishment was seen, if at all, as a separate phenomenon, unconnected to anything else. Pollution of air and water was one thing, family breakup and "loss of traditional values" another, violence and crime a third, and so forth. This compartmentalization made it virtually impossible to see any connection between the "positive" phenomenon called "growth" and the simultaneous *growth* of negative phenomena.

During this period of major party collaboration, many important questions might have been raised about economic growth. Is everything that was being called "growth" in fact socially desirable? Even if desirable, are there hidden costs that offset the gains? Even if growth is both desirable and not offset by costs, does it result in the neglect of other essential areas such as the personal sector? Is growth limited to the organized sector of society—to the System itself—allowing neglect to accumulate in the unorganized areas? Is growth limited to the measurable and the tangible while intangibles, such as the natural environment, loyalty, trust, or social cohesion in the human ecosystem, are being shattered? Is growth reaching a stage where it begins to reduce rather than increase employment, thereby creating a class of "surplus" people whose unemployment adds to profits? Is growth reaching a stage where it ceases to benefit the majority of working people and instead creates a more and more extreme inequality?

Despite these many unasked and unanswered questions, only a few thinkers have suggested that "growth" might present a false picture. One was the maverick British economist E. J. Mishan, who warned that what other economists called "externalities," such as pollution or congestion, were being ignored at our peril.[2] More recently, William D. Nordhaus and James Tobin introduced the term "Net Economic Welfare" to correct some of the errors in the Gross Domestic Product concept by subtracting certain costs of environmental damage and adding some values, such as leisure, not included in the GDP.[3]

Very recently, writing in the *Harvard Law Review*, Professor Cass R. Sunstein argues that economic growth is an inadequate measure of social well-being and that we need a "quality of life report" in addition. Sunstein also points out that poverty and unemployment can increase at the same time that Gross Domestic Product increases. Sunstein writes that a quality of life report should include unemployment, poverty, income distribution, subjection to violent crime, and a "human development index" that would include life expectancy, literacy, and educational attainments. Sunstein notes that Scandinavian countries and the Netherlands have identified a series of variables reflecting quality of life, including housing, health, recreation, and political participation. In Sunstein's view, information about the quality of life would provide the people of democratic societies with a way of judging whether their governments were successfully addressing these issues.[4]

While welcome, these critiques of economic growth do not go far enough. A more sweeping critique might point out that the term "growth" is applied indiscriminately to economic activity without any attempt to consider whether the goal of that activity actually contributes to the health of society. Hence "growth" inevitably includes many categories that might be deemed a sign of society's ill health rather than well-being. Prison building is included in "growth." In some depressed rural areas there is vigorous competition for the opportunity to build a prison, with its promise of steady employment. The manufacture of guns and weapons of mass destruction is "growth." The expense of investigating official corruption is "growth." All the activity connected with the war on crime—more police, more prosecutors, more criminal courts, more cash payments to informers—is "growth." The cleanup of the *Exxon Valdez* oil spill is "growth." The sale of security devices for the homes of frightened families and the hiring of security guards by companies to prevent their executives from being kidnapped are "growth." The sale of films and pictures depicting violence, sadism, or pornography is "growth." Growth is indifferent to whether it contributes to or detracts from justice and democracy. Some of the highest growth countries in the world are those with the worst records on human rights. As presently defined, growth is entirely amoral.

The concept of growth has been defined in such a way as to maximally benefit the System and its managers, to the disadvantage of all less powerful interests. The managers have tied the concept of economic growth ever more closely to the well-being of the System rather than the well-being of society as a whole. Today, economic growth means the growth of the System and those who are well placed within the System. Today, economic growth is reaching a stage where it means the impoverishment of nearly everyone and everything else. When the evening news broadcasts the latest increase in growth, those in managerial or investment positions may celebrate; those lower down should begin to realize that every percentage point of "growth" is a loss for them, for society, and for the environment.

The greatest flaw in the concept of economic growth is its failure to include a realistic view of costs. The economics profession, the chief intellectual sponsor of "growth," has entirely failed to develop an adequate concept of costs to accompany the idea of growth. And economics textbooks pay surprisingly little attention to costs. This silence serves to disguise and conceal the negative side of growth. What we call moral and social pathology—urban decay, crime, violence, family breakup, and all the rest—should instead be seen as costs. By failing to treat these negative phenomena as costs, their linkage to growth is denied, and the pathology seems to be the fault of individuals. The negative side of growth is thus rendered invisible.

All during the postwar decades of "high growth," the natural environment was suffering a largely unnoticed decline as toxic substances polluted air, soil, and water; species were driven to extinction; forests and watersheds were denuded; and natural resources were recklessly depleted. But these losses were never considered to be *costs* that should be *subtracted* from growth before reaching a realistic view of the nation's balance sheet. When a previously untapped natural resource such as an ancient forest is turned into commercially valuable logs or pulp, economists record a gain in wealth without any offsetting loss, refusing to treat the disappearance of the forest as a loss. In economic thinking, the unpolluted air and the unlogged forest have no measurable value until they are converted to a commercial use. Development is seen as a plus without any minus. As for values such as beauty or tranquillity, they cannot be quantified and therefore can be ignored, at least in economic thinking.

The spotted owl controversy is not so much about one endangered species as it is about the philosophy of growth as illustrated by the cutting down of irreplaceable ancient forest for short-term economic gain. The many values of the forest—biological diversity, watershed protection, beauty, spiritual value, and uniqueness—cannot be measured in dollars and cents. When "preservation" is pitted against monetary gain, the odds are stacked against the unmeasurable values. But to see the cutting down of such a forest as pure profit and economic growth, without subtracting the lost values of the forest, is a dangerous denial of reality. The nation has been keeping false account books.

A good example of keeping false account books is how we think about accidents and catastrophes such as oil spills and tanker truck explosions. Instead of seeing these events as predictable costs of economic activity, we are likely to seek an explanation in human error. A person is blamed, while the economic activity itself is exonerated. We continue to be surprised and shocked no matter how many times the same accident is repeated. Sight-seeing flights over the Grand Canyon are promoted as "growth." When the sight-seeing planes crash, it's an "accident." There have been at least eleven fatal air crashes and midair collisions at the Grand Canyon, leaving aircraft debris and human bodies scattered over formerly unspoiled areas.[5] What is the true cost of this particular form of "growth"?

Injury to the natural environment inflicts unmeasurable but very real costs on human beings, not just upon nature. At Yosemite, crowding and commercialization have turned the valley floor into an urban ghetto complete with pollution and crime. Debris from careless climbers has sullied once-pristine mountaintops, including Everest and Aconcagua, the highest peak in South America. Pollution has contaminated some of the best and most beautiful surfing areas in Southern California; at Santa Barbara, the beaches and ocean waters are spotted with globs of crude oil from nearby drilling platforms. The oil adheres to skin and clothing and is nearly impossible to remove. Forests suffer from what the Germans call the *Waldsterben* or forest-death, caused by a combination of toxic chemicals. The pure water of mountain lakes is contaminated by gasoline slicks and odors left by noisy speedboats. All of this defilement of nature subtracts from human enjoyment, health, and connection to the sacred. But we fail to count any of this as losses or costs attributable to growth.

When the existence of such costs is denied and the activities that cause them are absolved of responsibility, then these costs and their consequences escape from all control and become a lawless element in society, set free to cause wanton damage anywhere,

literally above the law. The Constitution of the State of
New York, in a justly famous and farsighted provision,
declares that the lands of the state constituting the
Forest Preserve shall be kept forever as wild forest
land, and the trees thereon shall not be sold, removed,
or otherwise destroyed. But in recent years this constitutional safeguard has been violated by air pollution
from sources far outside the park. The trees are visibly
being destroyed over large areas of wilderness. So long
as the pollution is not acknowledged as a cost for which
someone or something is responsible, the damage cannot be stopped and the constitutional safeguard is nullified. Such *rogue costs* become malignant agents of
destructive social change. This is what happens when
"growth" is presented as essentially cost-free, thereby
severing the negative effects of growth from its benefits
and allowing the damage to seem unexplainable.

Whether or not growth is deemed beneficial, and
whether or not growth rests on hidden costs, economic
growth presents a larger problem: It competes with the
human habitat just as it competes with the natural
habitat. The crisis of the family is one of the major
issues driving America's search for change. But where
does the threat to family and to family values come
from? A strong case can be made that economic
growth, rather than individual failure, plays the most
important role. Creating and maintaining a family requires much time and effort on the part of those in-

volved. But as feminists, among others, have pointed out, unpaid family labor is not counted as part of Gross Domestic Product. On the other hand, if both parents work outside the home, their earnings are counted as part of the GDC. These two kinds of labor necessarily compete with each other. But because family work is unpaid, it is at a great disadvantage in this competition. Economic necessity drives parents to seek paid work outside the home, no matter how much they might prefer to take care of their children and do the work of maintaining a home and family.

Of course, it has always been true that family work is unpaid—so what has changed? One major change is that two parents are likely to work outside the home today, whereas one breadwinner was sufficient in earlier times. To some degree, this change reflects the desire of women to have their own careers. But economic necessity also plays a major part. A single income is often insufficient to support a family today, whereas it was sufficient forty years ago. The value of one person's labor has been reduced relative to the cost of housing, food, transportation, health care, and other essentials. Many of these costs are beyond the control of individuals. People must work harder to keep up. The rising costs which individuals must face are all a part of economic growth.

The increasing disparity between what individuals can earn and what they must pay for necessities reflects the growth of the organized sector of the economy at the expense of the personal sector. Such *organizations* as public utilities; suppliers of transportation, housing, and health; and other producers of goods and services that people need are disproportionately the beneficiaries of economic growth. Their size and power allows them to increase their share of wealth relative to that of individuals. Because families are part of the personal sector, the well-being of families declines as the economic power of individuals declines. Since economic growth increases the power of organizations, it is damaging to those values and institutions which exist outside of the organization. Just as the mom-and-pop retail store cannot compete with Safeway, the mom-and-pop family cannot compete with the organized sector.

The personal sector includes many functions other than the family. But most of these activities, such as the habit of reading or the enjoyment of solitude, are little noticed by society as a whole and could disappear entirely without any outcry from politicians and self-appointed defenders of "traditional values." Indeed, the beleaguered domain of the personal is currently under attack by those who believe that there are too many individual rights and insufficient deference to authority. The family is the one function of the personal sector that excites society's concern. The outcry over the family obscures the fact that the personal sector as a whole is endangered. *Every* aspect of personal life is losing out to the organized sector.

In the competition between the personal sector and the organized sector, the family and other aspects of personal life receive the same economic treatment as the natural environment: They are accorded no monetary value and their loss is not counted as a cost. Despite all the pro-family talk, the family is treated exactly the same as the ancient forest in the Pacific Northwest. When the family is damaged or destroyed, we do not consider that the nation is economically any poorer. Thus families, like forests, fall victim to one-sided thinking about economic growth.

The family is also a victim of the devaluation of labor. Without a job, fathers flee their responsibilities, and when hard work brings in less than the cost of living, families suffer. Yet damage to family is not considered a *cost* of layoffs or low wages. Again, there is no one left to blame but individuals.

In April 1994 the Carnegie Corporation reported on a three-year study of the nation's young children. According to a front-page story in the *New York Times*, millions of infants and toddlers are so severely deprived of essential care that their development into healthy adults is seriously threatened. The United States ranks near the bottom of industrialized nations in providing services to help parents overwhelmed by poverty, teenage pregnancy, divorce, or work. The report "paints a bleak picture of disintegrating families, persistent poverty, high levels of child abuse, inadequate health care, and child care of such poor quality that it threatens youngsters' intellectual and emotional development."[6] One panel member commented, "Collectively, we all have to say, 'Enough.' " But enough of what? The report should have said, "Enough of one-sided growth."

If we want to understand the decline of the family, we must recognize how seriously disadvantaged it is by the present System. While individual effort can overcome these disadvantages some of the time, in other instances individual effort inevitably fails, and the overall decline of family continues. The distress of families represents the same kind of habitat loss already experienced by nonhuman life forms.

If our economy has reached a stage where it is damaging our own habitat, not just the habitats of other species, would we be aware of this? Damage to our own habitat might be very hard to recognize. Damage to plant and animal habitats shows up as loss of food supply, loss of nesting sites, difficulties with the reproductive cycle. Injury to human habitat and damage to human nature may be far more subjective and difficult to see than injury to the rest of nature. It is always harder to see what is happening to *us*. The great network of relationships that is an essential part of the human ecosystem is largely invisible. For example, the

element of *trust* in our relationships with each other
and with society is invisible, yet the loss of trust profoundly changes the way we live. It would be difficult
to "prove" that the element of trust in human relationships has been damaged by economic growth. It is far
easier for scientists to show that the eggshells of per-
egrine falcons have been damaged by DDT.

What would damage to the human habitat actually
look like to those within? What are the human equiva-
lents of the crucial relationships found in nature? When
we see the spread of loneliness and social isolation, the
breakdown of family ties, are we not seeing something
very much like the loss of habitat? When jobs disappear,
humans are in the same situation as animals whose
food supply vanishes. Our failure to see the similarity is
the product of compartmentalization. We place nature
in one compartment, human society in a separate compartment. Hence we fail to imagine that what injures
nature is capable of being injurious to us.

The most crucial part of any ecosystem—plant,
animal, or human—is how each life form makes its
living. For most human beings, livelihood is represented by a job. Therefore the relationship of individual to employer is central to the human ecosystem. It
represents our greatest dependency. Even those who
do not hold a job, such as children or a homemaker,
share in the dependence upon an employer. Although
unemployment is a significant factor in American life,

the great majority are employed, and it is *employment,* not unemployment, that can tell us the most about changes in American society.

The crucial role of the employer-employee relationship is the culmination of a long development. Today, the employer controls the livelihood of most people. And employment has come to represent much more than livelihood, vital though livelihood itself may be. A job represents our role in society, our place in the scheme of things. It determines our worth and status in social and psychological as well as financial terms. It defines us. It is a primary basis of citizenship and participation in the community. It not only puts food on the table and shelter over our heads, it is *what we do.* It is at the core of identity. And the workplace is a world—a world where we spend some of our most significant time. In many ways, the employer *is* society, or its representative.

Once employment has become essential to survival as the sole available source of livelihood and belonging, the employer is placed in a position of almost total power over the lives, ambitions, and status of fellow human beings. The efforts of employees to offset this total power by organizing unions has lost ground because most employees are readily replaceable. Today, the employer reigns supreme and a job has become the greatest single possession and necessity for any individual.

The record of how this power over livelihood has been used is now clear. During a period of almost continuous "growth," the vast majority of employees have been compelled to give up more and more. As the organized economy surged forward, the majority of employees have steadily and inexorably lost ground. They have lost ground in purely economic terms, and they have lost ground in ways equally important but less easily measured, such as security, dignity, and sense of belonging. They are forced into an unending struggle that pits their stagnant earnings and declining status against an array of rising costs they cannot control.

Employers are using their power to push more and more employees down below the level where they can share in the benefits of economic growth. It is this action, more than any other, that has created the discontent of the middle class, the anger at government, the mistrust of the elite. Of course, this is not the independent decision of individual employers; they are forced to go along with the economic system as a whole. It is the System that has made use of the employment power in the way just described. It is the System that has chosen to treat most employees as if they were parts of machines rather than parts of society, regardless of the social consequences of this policy.

The erosion of the security and dignity of most

working Americans might look to an observer outside
our society just as the disappearance of the habitat of
an animal or plant looks to us. Hard-working employees are asked to take pay cuts and reductions in benefits, to accept part-time or temporary work, or to work
for pay that is lower than what it costs a family to live
on. The more they work, the more they fall behind.
Companies have sharply reduced their commitment
and loyalty to employees, sending the message that
they are disposable and replaceable, firing older workers and hiring younger ones at lower pay.

These changes have severely damaged the elements of trust and commitment in the employment
relationship. In 1993, Michael and Rhonda Rawlins
lost their high-skilled jobs at Aetna Life. "It changes
your world, your sense of security," says Mrs. Rawlins
after thirteen years of employment. "People used to
feel a lot of loyalty and security there. It is just not that
way any more." Richard Freeman, a Harvard labor
economist, comments, "You ask who feels insecure
about their jobs and in every group, 80 percent of the
hands go up. That insecurity is the underlying reason
for the lack of wage pressure today."[7]

> When Bill, Jim, Carlos and Dave talk about
> mergers, they talk about lying awake at
> night. They talk about personal relationships
> souring under the strain of the same old

questions asked a hundred times. They talk about putting off vacations. They talk about feeling lost in the shuffle.

Bill [is a] 42-year-old Vietnam veteran who vacillates between anger and astonishment that life has been reduced to this level of uncertainty. "How do you stop thinking about it? How do you get away from it? There ain't enough Maalox."[8]

Besides creating insecurity and a downward standard of living for the many, growth also is based upon ever-greater inequality. Corporations enhance their profits by creating a two-tier labor force, with those in the lower tier unable to escape poverty or make ends meet even though they work full-time. According to a report in the *Los Angeles Times*,

Poverty, long the scourge of the underclass, is rising like an evil tide to engulf the "working poor"—thousands upon thousands of Americans who hold down regular jobs and struggle to embrace the traditional values of middle-class society, but find themselves sinking despite their best efforts.

Millions of others, although technically living above the poverty line, have little more than bare necessities and struggle with illiteracy, homelessness, crime, disease, and all the other afflictions of the poor. So fragile is their grip on the economic ladder that the slightest jolt can be disastrous.[9]

Economic growth has always been considered synonymous with jobs. In the struggle between environmentalists and proponents of development, the argument of the pro-growth forces is always "jobs, jobs, jobs." Every tax break for business and every other form of governmental assistance to business is inevitably justified by the promise of jobs. That growth produces jobs is an unquestioned assumption of every economic debate and decision. Nevertheless, during the fifty years of nearly continuous growth, some of it spectacular, since World War II, another phenomenon has also grown—a persistent "underclass," a permanent class of the unemployed.

Conservatives have put forward the thesis that the underclass is a product of individual moral and cultural failure, sustained by the dependency created by welfare. According to conservatives, the remedy is to end the welfare system and require members of the underclass to work. This thesis turns the true story upside down. Welfare and dysfunctional behavior did not come first. What came first was the steady downward pressure on the earnings of the workforce, plus the total exclusion of more and more people desperate to earn a living. Today's "underclass" is the outgrowth of the economy's inability to provide jobs for millions of those who seek them, plus racial discrimination, plus the post–World War II abandonment of New Deal jobs programs. This left only welfare for the unemployed. Permanent exclusion from the economy, disconnection from mainstream society, and rejection by the society are far more potent causes of pathology, resignation, and despair than welfare. The underclass is not primarily a "cultural" phenomenon but an economic one—the direct consequence of an economy which consigns millions of people to the status of the unwanted, unused, and discarded.

It is economic deprivation that comes first, dysfunctional behavior second, in the true cause-and-effect sequence. A *New York Times* article reports:

> As the unemployment rate continues to climb, each month hundreds of thousands of Americans discover that involuntary joblessness is often more of an emotional and physical challenge than any job they have ever held.
>
> . . . many studies have shown or strongly suggested that unemployment breeds a host of personal, family, and social ills, from depression and heart attacks to child abuse and criminal violence.[10]

European workers report the emotional impact of joblessness. Laid off British autoworker David Doidge, forty, says: "The worst is the boredom. I need a job to feel like I'm someone again." "You feel so useless," said Victor Hearn, nineteen, who lost his apprenticeship in a small metal factory. "It's like you're trash, nothing. Nobody wants you."[11]

In a study of families of autoworkers who had recently lost or were expecting to lose their jobs, job loss was associated with increased household conflict, tension, and stress. The unemployed workers were more likely to have fights with their spouses, and to have hit, slapped, or spanked their children. Unemployed workers were also more likely to suffer from severe headaches, chronic nausea, stomach troubles, and constant fatigue.[12]

The underclass is indeed the result of a moral failure—but not that of the unfortunate victims of our economy. The true moral failure is exemplified by the refusal of Congress to raise the minimum wage above the starvation level, the readiness of the Federal Reserve Board to maintain a high level of unemployment by repeatedly raising interest rates, and the failure of economists to treat unemployment and the human damage it causes as costs that should be subtracted from "growth." The true moral failure is our refusal as a society to recognize that when the livelihood and habitat of human beings is destroyed, damage results that no effort of individual willpower can overcome.

When their habitat is destroyed, plants and animals simply perish. With human beings, the consequences are not so simple. Human beings may remain alive but be subjected to fundamental damage to behavior and character. Aspects of what makes a human being may be defective or missing. Vital connections between people, emotions such as empathy and compassion, may be suppressed or never even be developed. Control over angry and violent impulses may be impaired. When we observe the social pathology of America today, including everything from the extraordinary level of violence to the breakdown of family connections, we see a vast, new, unprecedented phenomenon: the visible consequence of the destruction of human habitat and relationships. As we destroy the human habitat, we see the rise of deranged behavior.

The mote in our eye is our need to place blame on individuals for their "failure" or their antisocial behavior. In contrast, we are far less judgmental concerning the pathology of plants and animals. Few of us would insist that "blame" is the best way to improve the health of plants or animals. Most of us realize that a tree or bird or fish that begins to self-destruct because of toxic chemicals in the atmosphere is part of a larger problem. Not even the threat of life imprisonment without possibility of parole for a bird, or twenty lashes with a rattan cane for a tree, can be expected to bring about a positive alteration in their condition.

It would be folly to punish animals or trees for their condition, because they are not willfully responsible for what is happening to them. *They are dying,* and dying cannot be halted by threats of punishment. If we were to consider for just a moment that the poverty, violence, addiction, extreme selfishness, and lack of self-control by people in this society is symptomatic of the fact that our ecosystem is being destroyed and *we are dying,* then we might not be so insistent that such human behavior can be deterred or reformed at the individual level.

If we look objectively at the behavior that constitutes social breakdown, we should recognize that although much of it threatens others and society, it is primarily self-destructive and indicative of neglect, damage, and an inability to function. Senseless violence, crimes by younger and younger children, children having children, fatherless families—all suggest the actions of human beings in a state of chaos. One of the most widely noted and feared forms of "new behavior" is a wanton disregard for the value of human life, demonstrated by violence that goes beyond what is necessary to achieve any rational purpose and treats human beings as indifferently as inanimate objects. A family is wiped out when a speeding automobile appears out of nowhere on a residential street; the driver was wantonly indifferent to other human lives. A store owner hands over all of his money to a young robber—and gets fatally shot anyway. Week by week, unprecedented departures from the expected limits of human behavior are reported. It is almost as if a "new and improved model" of criminal had appeared—unpredictable, without apparent motive, not given to rational calculation of self-interest, nondeterrable by any known means of deterrence.

There are many descriptions that might be given to this "new product." It is apparent that we are dealing with a profound form of dehumanization plus *disconnection*, the increasing isolation of one human being from another. When we look for forces that might be causing dehumanization, we are brought back to the economic system. Dehumanization is characteristic of large organizations, including corporations and government. The triumph of the organizational form is due to its "efficiency." In turn, this efficiency stems from making people into machine-parts, used for specific skills and disposed of when these skills are no longer needed. Executives of organizations must be able to distance themselves from workers they transfer or terminate according to the needs of the organization. In short, the disconnected individual is based on the model of a person who contributes services to the System, but whose other human qualities are not valued. When this person is no longer of use, she is terminated.

Thirty years ago the anthropologist Jules Henry, in *Culture Against Man,* wrote that ". . . America's industrial progress has made many people spiritually useless to themselves." Economic pressures require a worker to accept work that means giving up an essential part of himself, which is ". . . pushed down with all his other unmet needs to churn among them for the rest of his life . . . selves have been ground up by the technological system. . . ." According to Henry, the economy relies on fear ". . . of competition, of failure, of loss of markets, of humiliation, of becoming obsolete. . . ." The final result of this cultural process is madness. "We are as highly developed in psychopathology as in technology. . . . Psychosis is the final outcome of all that is wrong with a culture . . . parents, blinded by their own disorientation, confusion, and misery, sometimes half mad themselves, make dreadful mistakes. . . . How can a parent who is psychologically blind perceive what he did to his child? . . . Culture is a unified whole, even unto psychosis and death."[13]

The process of personal disintegration described by Jules Henry has been enormously intensified by the extremes of power and powerlessness engendered by the System and their consequences. Ashley Montagu and Floyd Matson write:

> For most persons the dead weight of powerlessness is experienced directly as a private burden, a debilitating factor in the increas-

ingly stressful task of getting through the
day—and making it through the night. . . .
Our subjective feelings of helplessness—of
the absence of choice, the futility of effort,
the loss of control, the failure of nerve—are
graphically reinforced by the printouts from
the laboratories of behavioral science. Thus
the psychiatric code words for powerlessness—depression,   anxiety,   impotence,
rage—describe a condition so common as to
seem epidemic among us.[14]

Consider the profound conflict between the dependency, subjugation, and submission experienced in
the workplace and the socialization of males in our
society, which requires that they be domineering, ag-
gressive, and value winning above everything else. All
too often men forced into a submissive role at work
will be driven to play an inappropriately domineering
role at home. Filled with anger, they hurt those dependent upon them. Recently, we have read about young
men who habitually beat their girlfriends. According
to a story in *Newsweek*, an eighteen-year-old said, "It's
because you've got anger inside."[15] Beatings in the
home, in which the coercive relationships of the economic world are reproduced, also serve as a first stage
in the making of violent criminals. Lonnie H. Athens
describes what she calls "violent subjugation." An authority figure in the home, usually a father or stepfa-

ther, employs violence to force a child to comply with
a command. The victim's submission finally stops the
beating. But "[t]he humiliation from being brutally
beaten down incenses the subject. Her burning rage
becomes cooled only later when it is transformed into
a desire for revenge."[16]

We have built a machine for dehumanization of
such force and destructive power, through its cumula-
tive assaults on human dignity, that we are creating
kinds and degrees of damage to human beings beyond
anything ever known, with totally unforeseeable consequences. Dehumanization is undoubtedly an *aggre-
gate*, composed of many seemingly separate influences
which we ordinarily do not add together. Thus, inequality and insecurity, when added together, may be
much more potent than either is by itself. Inequality
generates anger; insecurity generates fear; but in combination they may generate something that is more
intense than the sum of the parts. The vertical extremes
between privileged and rejected in our society prevent
those at the top from knowing how much dehumanization takes place from the middle to the bottom. For
example, those at the top experience little or no coercion, and are often in a position to impose their will
upon others. Those at the bottom are always subject to
coercion, whether at low-status jobs or in dealing with
welfare authorities.

Our economic system inflicts profound psychological harm on people at the lower end of the eco-

nomic ladder by making them feel rejected and labeling them as "losers." The System makes people feel that they have been punished for lack of merit when, in fact, there are simply not enough good jobs to go around. People can endure a great deal of pain and deprivation if it is required by war or is seemingly ordained by fate, but here the suffering may well be the result of inequality, injustice, and betrayal of promises. It is understandable that many feel they have been sorted out for failure by a process over which they had little control and which was inherently unfair. To make matters even worse, the sorting is accompanied by an unmistakable message that unwanted workers are trash, they are disposable, they are not part of the community. There is much about the System that fills a parental role for most of us; rejection and exclusion thus have the added sting of feeling as if they originated with an all-powerful but uncaring parent. We all know that even the smallest and most trivial rejection can hurt. What of a massive rejection that is also unjust, unfair, and inflicts continuing deprivation? Society has built elaborate machinery for selecting, praising, and lavishing gifts upon a small group of winners. But this same process results in rejecting, discarding, scorning, and punishing a much larger group of "losers."

To be thrust outside in this society does not mean to be free of restraint. On the contrary, it means finding oneself in an *outside prison* where coercion, ugliness, pollution, and violence are everywhere, and from which, without money, escape is impossible. The homeless person is deprived of liberty and dignity. How is citizenship possible for a person who has no place, physical or psychological, within society?

Environmentalists have learned that there is a kind of biological shock that can be delivered to a species or to an entire ecosystem by the combined effect of many pollutants, invasions, and other injuries. Today we have a form of "economic death" visited upon people in the midst of plenty and under circumstances which deny all worth and dignity to the sufferers. The combination of all of these factors acting together on a human being has not been studied, is not understood, and may well be very much greater than anyone imagines, including the sufferers, who may indeed blame themselves and deny their own pain.

Economic growth has become separated from the needs of human beings and the human community. The more growth proceeds along this separate path, the more conflict it creates. Why is this happening? We must recognize that an exclusive reliance on economic and organizational efficiency produces a conflict model of society. Economic efficiency dictates that labor costs be cut whenever possible, forcing more and more working people into lower paying, less secure jobs or forcing them out of the economy altogether. Organizational efficiency has been the basis for a greater and greater concentration of power at the top. When society itself comes to be modeled on these economic and organizational principles, all of the forces that bind people together are torn apart in the struggle for survival, community is destroyed, and we are no longer "in this together" because everyone is a threat to everyone else. In the long run, the conflict model of a society is not efficient at all, because the costs of exclusion and divisiveness become enormous, and because there are fewer and fewer people able to afford the goods that are produced. Indeed, an atmosphere of pervasive conflict encourages every form of racial, religious, and class hatred as group is pitted against group; it encourages violence and crime, and it strips people of kindness and compassion as these qualities become disadvantageous in an ever more warlike atmosphere.

As conflict increases, America's historic effort to achieve a politics of inclusion becomes more and more difficult to maintain. In recent decades a new politics has emerged, one that no longer seeks to represent all of the interests in society or to reconcile their differences. This new politics actually *embraces* conflict and promotes divisiveness. By setting people against each other, by permitting insecurity, fear, and even hatred to fester, the System's control can be strengthened. Seeing each other as the enemy, individuals and groups use up their energy in fighting each other, while each turns to the System for help and advantage.

Many governments and many nations have sought to gain strength by having an enemy—outside or internal—to serve as a focus for discontent and blame. The System has taken this familiar way of ruling and given it new life by *producing* an enemy class in the form of the growing number of people who are excluded or forced downward. By this method, an abundance of enemies is always present and a fresh supply is always on the way.

There is a point at which a line is crossed between the reluctant acceptance of conflict as a by-product of otherwise beneficial growth, and the embrace and promotion of conflict as a way of instilling fear and remaining in power. The moment of crossing can be identified as the point where one side of the conflict is deprived of its legitimacy and voice.

This active promotion of conflict is the end product of economic growth that takes place at the expense of the needs of human beings and of the connections which bind society together. The costs which we deny and the needs which we repress rise up in unrecognizable and uncontrollable alien forms, threatening us like terrifying monsters. Crime, drugs, violence, the underclass, and rampant selfishness become an invading enemy, not the product of our own System for which we must take responsibility. As the illusion of outside invaders becomes uncannily real, we are drawn into an ever more destructive war against ourselves.

4

THE
GREAT
LAWBREAKER

Among the many human needs disregarded by the System, the need for justice occupies a special place. The human desire for justice, for fairness, for observance of the fundamental law, can be as urgent as hunger and thirst. Justice is a need for which people throughout history have been willing to sacrifice their lives and possessions. Justice binds human beings together in a community or nation; injustice destroys the social fabric and ultimately leads to revolution. Of all the damage caused by our present System, perhaps the greatest is its destruction of justice, fairness, and our constitutional compact.

The institutions designed to protect justice, led by the Supreme Court of the United States, have tragically failed in their primary duty to the American people. This is no accident. The great judicial figures of our past have been replaced by mid-level bureaucrats carefully screened to assure their loyalty to the System. Their seal of approval upon the many wrongs of the System has desecrated the marble temple where they sit and brought confusion and cynicism to the trusting people who look to the Court for "Equal Justice Under Law."

The wrongs of the System are the deepest source of our present national discontent. Unlike the wrongs of individuals, the wrongs of the System are difficult to recognize because they are large in scale, result from the combined actions of many officials, none of whom are held personally responsible, and involve the violation of basic obligations of society to its members which the System denies. For example, the Constitution provides that no person shall be denied life, liberty, or property without due process of law, a guarantee that goes back nearly eight hundred years to Magna Carta (1215). When a person in our centrally managed economy is denied an opportunity to earn a living despite being fully qualified and ready to work, this guarantee has been violated— whether the supine Supreme Court says so or not. The Constitution also provides that no person shall be denied the "equal protection of the laws." When our managed economy forces a whole class of citizens, including children, to go without the basic necessities of life in a society wealthy enough to provide for all, and when this discrimination is disproportionately based upon race and upon deprivation of publicly funded educational opportunities which others enjoy, the constitutional guarantee of equality has been violated, and we do not have to wait for the Court to tell us that this is so. When the State is the lawbreaker, we cannot depend upon the State's own institutions to uphold the law. On the question of the System's wrongdoing, it is the citizen who must be the judge.

The wrongs of the System range over many areas, from the political, where people have been deprived of power over their own lives and over the decisions made by the System, to the area of knowledge, where people have been denied an explanation of how they are governed. If we limit our focus to just one area—the economic—the charges against the System might read as follows:

1. The System has breached the social contract with the American people, in force since the Great Depression, under which the people delegated new powers to government for the purpose of managing the economy *fairly and equitably in the interest of the nation as a whole*. The System has also breached the social contract by failing in its obligation to provide adequate support to people who, through no fault of their own, are denied access to economic opportunity.

2. The System has used its control over livelihood to force a large segment of the population
to work for rates of pay and under conditions
that they would never accept of their own free
will. Although they work full time, they are paid
less than the minimum cost of housing, food,
medical care, and the other essentials of life. The
work they are required to perform is often dehumanizing, demeaning, dangerous to physical
and mental health, and offers neither present
security nor future hope. The System has also
used its control over livelihood to prevent a large
segment of the population from making any
living at all. They are excluded from the economic community. They are denied the freedom
to exchange their labor—their only asset—for
the goods and services they need to survive. The
value of their labor has been confiscated by the
System to benefit others.

3. Both of these segments of the population have
been condemned to live in poverty—a form of internal exile—where they exist in dangerous and
despairing zones of cities, lacking all of the freedoms that require money to buy, and deprived of
the forms of support, such as dignity, approval,
and encouragement, that enable human beings to
flourish and be part of a community. Poverty is an

unnecessary and artificial condition, because the
economy has ample means to include everyone in
a reasonable standard of living.

4. The System has used its control over livelihood to divide people into classifications representing extreme inequality. The classifications
include both forms of poverty—poverty by exclusion and poverty by substandard pay—and lead
up to a very small classification of people at the
top who possess an unconscionable surplus of
support and wealth. The inequality is said to be
based upon merit, but in fact people are selected
for both the high and low classifications on the
basis of factors such as family background, race,
gender, and sexual orientation that are unfair, irrational, and unjustifiable. The resulting inequality cuts across every area of life, including access
to nature, physical and psychic well-being, equality before the law, and ability to participate in
democratic self-government.

5. The System has allowed employers to exercise
governmental powers over employees without requiring that these powers be subject to the Bill of
Rights. Employers have limited the free speech
rights of employees, they invade employee privacy
by surveillance and random drug testing, and em-

ployers terminate employees without notice or hearing even after years of service. In consequence, the employee's status as a subordinate supersedes the citizen's status as sovereign.

6. The System has attempted to contain the human consequences of economic injustice by imprisoning one and a half million individuals, almost all of whom are from the lowest economic classes with minorities in disproportionate numbers. The System, with help from the courts, has damaged beyond recognition the constitutional guarantee of fair play in the criminal justice system, including the procedural safeguards of the Bill of Rights. The System has created new criminal laws aimed directly at the poor.

7. The System has used its power over communications to prevent the whole subject of its control over livelihood, and the ways it has exercised that power, from being discussed and debated. The entire subject of the System's duties and obligations to the people it is supposed to serve has been excluded from public discussion. Discussion of morality and right and wrong does not include wrongs and violations of fundamental law by the System. The poor are blamed for their condition and given no opportunity to reply.

The background of this indictment is as follows.
Our society rests upon a constitutional contract between the people and their government. The contract
creates a government of carefully limited powers and
leaves individuals free to pursue economic self-
sufficiency, liberty, and happiness in a world where
these are attainable goals. But in today's economy only
a few people are economically self-sufficient; whole areas of life that used to support self-sufficiency, such as
farming and craftsmanship, have virtually disap-
peared; and livelihood is now possible for the majority
of individuals only by accepting a dependent position—a job. Most people can no longer rely on land or
skill or property to support their independence and
have only the security (or lack of it) that a job affords.

We have accepted and grown accustomed to this
profound change of circumstances in exchange for the
immense benefits of organized, technological society
where economic efficiency rules and a far higher standard of living is possible than in agrarian society. But
in our new economically vulnerable position, our independence is at risk from forces and decisions we
cannot control. When millions were thrown out of
work in the Great Depression, government assumed a
measure of responsibility for social protection, thus
negotiating a "new deal" or new version of the old contract. What emerged was a "deal" in which government
took responsibility for seeing that the economy did not

treat the people who had become dependent upon it too harshly or too unfairly. It is this obligation that the System is wrongfully failing to honor.

The *Wall Street Journal*, in a front-page story by Tony Horwitz, dated December 1, 1994, describes how some of the "growth jobs" of the nineties are totally incompatible with individual freedom. In the poultry processing industry, for example, assembly-line workers labor under cramped, unsanitary, hazardous conditions. Having received a modicum of training, they must perform monotonous tasks at a rapid speed, risking their health at a wage of $5 an hour. These employees are subject to harsh work rules, company-imposed restrictions on doctor visits and injury claims, and usually lack labor union representation. Similarly, in another American "growth industry," clerical workers who process charity donations are given mind-numbing tasks with high-pressure quotas in exchange for low wages and few benefits. While they silently toil in windowless rooms—forbidden to talk, decorate their desks, or take any break except for lunch—they are closely monitored by video cameras and daily print-outs of their errors.

Horwitz characterizes these jobs as "work that is faster than ever before, subject to Orwellian control and electronic surveillance, and reduced to limited tasks that are numbingly repetitive, potentially crippling and stripped of any meaningful skills or the chance to develop them." These jobs pay the lowest possible wages and yet represent the best or only employment available for many Americans. Grueling work for eight hours or more, with permission required even to go to the bathroom, strains the limits of human endurance. Safety violations and injuries are often ignored. Years of hard labor lead to no better future. "While American industry reaps the benefit of a new, high-technology era, it has consigned a large class of workers to a Dickensian time warp, laboring not just for meager wages but also under dehumanizing and often dangerous conditions."[1]

There is a fundamental difference between conditions, however harsh, that are created by nature or by unfettered economic activity, and conditions that result from the exercise of governmental power. The same conditions that we can accept as resulting from the unregulated play of impersonal forces become unacceptable when they derive from the exercise of powers that are meant to be used for the benefit of society as a whole. If the economy, once it has been entrusted to managers, is managed in such a way that work for many becomes a form of involuntary servitude—expressly outlawed by the Constitution—then such conditions constitute tyranny. If the economy has been managed in such a way that a significant percentage of our youth, filled with faith in the American dream and hopes for a life of promise and meaning, are condemned instead to the bitterness and hopelessness of work without security, dignity, or a future, we should also call that tyranny. If the economy is managed so that a lifetime of hard work produces no security, no relief from the worries of old age, and if even that lifetime of work can be cut short at any moment by a dismissal that is like a sentence of economic death, that too is tyranny.

It is one thing to accept the necessity of working together with many others in large organizations; it is another thing entirely if that work is made humiliating, demeaning, and lacking in dignity. Work must not be turned into punishment nor forced on people for less than a living wage, nor should people be required to work under conditions that are soul-destroying. Use of economic power to create unjust, unfree, or inhuman conditions is a violation of the original social contract that promised genuine opportunity and independence. It is also a violation of the New Deal social contract under which centralized economic power was intended to benefit all.

The claim that government is free to reduce or cut off welfare and other forms of support for people in economic need is totally mistaken. Welfare is not a gift, nor is it, despite frequent assertions, a transfer from those who are earning a living to those who are not. Welfare is an obligation from society—and from those who are working—to those who have been deprived of work and the opportunity to earn a living. If we want to speak of transfers, it would be more accurate to say that those with a secure place in the economic system are enjoying a transfer of wealth from those who are excluded from the economic system. Welfare is partial compensation for a deprivation of livelihood that allows others to work.

The change in circumstances that requires support for those denied economic opportunity was recognized nationally more than sixty years ago, and has only recently been forgotten. In the 1932 presidential campaign, Franklin D. Roosevelt promised a "new deal," and that phrase was not just a slogan but a concept. In a speech given in San Francisco on September 23, 1932, Roosevelt described how changes in the nation's economy required new terms for the old social contract. We began, he said, with "the happiest of economic conditions." Land on the western frontier was available. "No one, who did not shirk the task of earning a living, was entirely without opportunity to do so." Despite economic ups and downs, "starvation and dislocation were practically impossible." When depression came, new land was opened up.

In the middle of the nineteenth century, Roosevelt continued, the industrial revolution brought a new dream—"of an economic machine, able to raise the standard of living for everyone; to bring luxury within the reach of the humblest . . . and to release everyone from the drudgery of the heaviest manual toil." But, said F.D.R., there was "a shadow over the dream." Along with the industrial revolution came giant corporations which threatened the economic freedom of individuals to earn a living. Roosevelt observed that when Woodrow Wilson was elected in 1912, Wilson saw, in the highly centralized economic system that was developing, "the despot of the twentieth century, on whom great masses of individuals relied for their safety and their livelihood, and whose irresponsibility and greed (if they were not controlled) would reduce them to starvation and penury.

"A glance at the situation today," Roosevelt continued after quoting Wilson, "only too clearly indicates that equality of opportunity as we have known it no longer exists." Roosevelt pointed out that the frontier had closed, that there was no more free land, that opportunities in business had narrowed, and "area after area has been preempted altogether by the great corporations. . . ." Recently, said F.D.R., a study of our economic life revealed that six hundred corporations controlled two thirds of American industry: "[I]f the process of concentration goes on at the same rate, at the end of another century we shall have all American industry controlled by a dozen corporations, and run by perhaps a hundred men. Put plainly, we are steering a steady course toward economic oligarchy, if we are not there already."

All of this, according to Roosevelt, calls for "a reappraisal of values." We need, he continued, to develop "an economic declaration of rights, an economic constitutional order. . . . It is the minimum requirement of a more permanently safe order of things." The Declaration of Independence, F.D.R. said, puts the problem of government in terms of a contract where those who are accorded power receive it subject to certain rights retained by the people. "I feel we are coming to a view . . . that private economic power . . . is a public trust as well. I hold that continued enjoyment of that power by any individual or group must depend upon the fulfillment of that trust." Roosevelt called this a "greater social contract," the terms of which "are as old as the Republic, and as new as the new economic order." Roosevelt described the new social contract as follows:

> Every man has a right to life; and this means that he also has a right to make a comfortable living. He may by sloth or crime decline to exercise that right; but it may not be denied him. We have no actual famine or dearth; our industrial and agricultural mechanism can produce enough and to spare. Our Government formal and informal, political and economic, owes to everyone an avenue to possess himself of a portion of that plenty sufficient for his needs, through his own work.

This requirement, Roosevelt said, is a responsibility of those who control the great industrial and financial combinations which dominate our economic life. "They have undertaken to be, not business men, but princes of property. I am not prepared to say that the system which produces them is wrong. I am very clear that they must fearlessly and competently assume the responsibility that goes with the power." We must fulfill "the new terms of the old social contract," Roosevelt concluded, "lest a rising tide of misery, engendered by our common failure, engulf us all."[2]

In his 1944 Annual Message to Congress, and in a Fireside Chat to the American people delivered the same evening (January 11, 1944), President Roosevelt provided a more complete version of the new social contract. After mentioning the American heritage of political rights, he continued: "We have come to a clearer realization of the fact, however, that true individual freedom cannot exist without economic security and independence. 'Necessitous men are not free men.' People who are hungry, people who are out of a job are the stuff of which dictatorships are made." Therefore, Roosevelt continued, as these economic truths have been accepted as self-evident, we must accept the justice of "a second Bill of Rights under which a new basis of security and prosperity can be established for all—regardless of station or race or creed."

The new social contract, Roosevelt said, must provide for security, and for human happiness and well-being. The new economic order would include:

> the right to a useful and remunerative job in the industries or shops or farms or mines of the nation;
> the right to earn enough to provide adequate food and clothing and recreation;
> the right of farmers to raise and sell their products at a return which will give them and their families a decent living;
> the right of every businessman, large and small, to trade in an atmosphere of freedom from unfair competition and domination by monopolies at home or abroad;
> the right of every family to a decent home;
> the right to adequate medical care and the opportunity to achieve and enjoy good health;
> the right to adequate protection from the economic fears of old age and sickness and accident and unemployment; and finally, the right to a good education.[3] "

As Roosevelt made clear, the reason for a new social contract was changed economic reality. Economic independence and equality of opportunity had been lost in the transition to the giant organizations of the economic machine. These organizations held power over the livelihood and economic security of individual Americans. In return for holding this power, they must provide what individuals can no longer provide independently. This was the "new deal."

Roosevelt's proposals were just a beginning for a revision of the social contract that should have been vigorously continued and added to in the post–World War II years as economic concentration rapidly increased. Because of this steady increase of centralized economic management, the obligations owed to individuals in 1962 or 1982 should have been much greater than in 1932. But not only was there no progress beyond F.D.R., his own new social contract was never fully enacted. Before World War II several parts of the new contract were adopted, such as Social Security. However, the central guarantee of livelihood was never acted upon. After World War II there were some important "Great Society" additions, such as Medicare. Nevertheless the new social contract lagged further and further behind economic realities. Meanwhile an immense new growth of inequality, never imagined in Roosevelt's time, took place.

The new economic edifice built after World War II created a society in the image of the corporate hierarchy. The economic hierarchy became a social hierarchy as well, creating well-defined social classes. The pyramid became high and steep. Those few at the top had work that was well compensated and fulfilling; those near the bottom experienced punishing work and economic deprivation. We have traditionally accepted inequality based on each individual's efforts and abilities. But today's inequality is different. Inequality is present in the structure of the economy before the individual arrives on the scene. If the structure is such that out of every 1,000 persons 10 percent will be jobless and homeless, another 20 percent will be desperately poor, and only 5 percent at the top will be comfortable and secure, then those who fill these preordained slots cannot be held fully responsible for their situation; they are caught in a game of musical chairs where it is guaranteed ahead of time that all but a few will be losers. Even if they are equally talented and deserving, 950 people out of 1,000 will still end up as losers, just as they would in a lottery. If the slots cannot be changed no matter how hard people strive, then the resulting inequality is the creation of the System, not of the effort or lack of effort by individuals.

When positions of privilege are dependent on educational advantages that only the privileged can obtain, then the top slots become inheritable, and both privilege and poverty become fixed from generation to generation. Worse yet is the fact that the "losers" are disparaged for their condition. In the fixed social systems of traditional aristocratic societies, at least those at the bottom are told that they are part of a hierarchy ordained by God and that their place is one of dignity. In contrast, we have a system that pretends that all 1,000 of us could and should be winners, and when that proves impossible, the losers cannot help but feel bitter disappointment, frustration, and rage.

Moreover, today's inequality results from a carefully managed selection process that starts in elementary school and condemns many children to the "slow track" before they even have a chance to develop. Supposedly based on "merit," actually based partly on tests and partly on socioeconomic background, this selection process takes place so early in life that it inherently favors those from already privileged backgrounds. By contrast, the "old inequality" was based not on educational achievements but on actual achievements as an adult. The many American success stories of individuals who never finished school would be virtually impossible today.

The "new inequality" is also much more extreme than the old. We now live in what has aptly been called a winner-take-all economy.[4] Both wealth and deprivation are driven to extremes. And inequality has a greater impact because so many of the important areas of life that once were free and open to all, such as access to nature, now cost money. Once any child could go fishing. For the child trapped in urban surroundings today, nature may be unavailable without money. In many other ways, the pleasures and necessities of life have been privatized.

Inequality has also come to mean a loss of freedom as well as a lack of wealth. The lower a person is on the economic scale, the more that coercion takes the place of freedom. People are driven by necessity, not choice. We should recognize that *economic coercion is really violence in slow motion*. If we are trying to find the causes of rising violence, we should recognize that economic coercion is on the rise, and it teaches people to do exactly what the System does—use force when they want something badly enough. The new inequality is both an unbearable injustice and the source of an explosive combination of fear and anger.

Beyond the issue of inequality, the System exercises undue political power through its administration of the workplace. The original Constitution and Bill of Rights applied limits only to the government, leaving the private employer free to make whatever rules he might desire. In theory, employees were free to accept the employer's conditions or seek employment elsewhere. Now that employees have little choice but to accept an employer's dictates, and those dictates have become governmental in nature, the situation is very different. For example, many employers require that employees submit to drug testing, thus helping the police to enforce the criminal laws. This cooperation of "private" employers with public government in a matter affecting the constitutional rights of employees shows why employer dictates should be subject to the Bill of Rights. The courts might have interpreted the Bill of

Rights in this way, but they have failed to do so. As a result, employers can and do invade employees' privacy on and off the job, enforcing a conformity that is at odds with democratic values. Thus, there is an urgent need to reinterpret or amend the Constitution so that it applies to large organizations that no longer deserve to be considered "private."

There is nothing at all about the work relationship that requires or justifies the treatment of employees as anything less than citizens. Freedom of speech, privacy, the right to choose one's own lifestyle, and freedom from personal searches and unreasonable surveillance are among the citizenship rights employers now frequently deny their employees. And employers may discipline or terminate employees without affording them the kind of fair treatment embodied in the constitutional concept of due process of law. These and other abuses of power by employers threaten the strength of our democracy.

The testing of employees for signs of drug use also illustrates how the denial of employee rights leads to unacceptable class distinctions that deny the equal protection of the laws. Company directors and top executives are not subjected to drug testing. Lawyers, doctors, and other professionals are not subjected to drug testing. Judges are not subjected to drug testing. These exceptions cannot be explained by logic. If drug testing is necessary to ensure that job performance is

unimpaired, then logic would require that those in positions of great responsibility ought to be tested along
with low-level employees. Why should entry-level employees be tested, while airline executives, surgeons,
and banking officials are not tested, although they are
responsible for the safety and well-being of the public?

The answer is that drug testing and other invasions of employee dignity and privacy are based upon
social class and power, not safety. Drug tests are first
and foremost a humiliation of "lower" people by
"higher" people who hold power over their "inferiors."
At a recent Supreme Court argument, Chief Justice
William Rehnquist openly scoffed at the claim of an
Oregon schoolboy that compulsory urine testing was
an invasion of privacy. If the Chief Justice were forced
to urinate into a receptacle in order to prove his com-
petence to serve, we would all understand that dignity is profoundly compromised by such procedures.
In a democracy, why should the dignity of a Supreme
Court justice be more important than the dignity of a
seventh grader?[5]

The wrongs of the System culminate in the increasing reliance on harsh criminal punishment to deal
with the human damage caused by the economy. It is
true that crime is not caused by economic deprivation
alone, although the two are closely linked. But the as-
tonishing rise of crime and incarceration during the
past forty years precisely parallels the rise of the Sys-

tem itself. If we look at *all* of the harmful changes brought about by the System, including political powerlessness, extreme inequality, starvation wages and exclusion from the economic community, tax relief for the wealthy, contemptuous treatment of the poor as "losers," coercion and dehumanization of those at the bottom of the ladder, destruction of habitat and community, and the ruthlessness with which workers are cast off when no longer wanted, we have a more than adequate explanation of how society creates crime, violence, and the desire for revenge. When we add to this the invisibility of the System and the calculated deception it practices, we can comprehend the paranoia that so often accompanies antisocial behavior. People who commit violent acts may not correctly identify the enemy, but they are correct in sensing that lawlessness and injustice begin at the top.

Crime may not be justifiable, but it is preventable—by a more equitable and humane management of the nation's economy. Crime overwhelmingly reflects the conditions under which people grow up. Our prisons are not filled with middle-class persons who went bad. People with a good job and a comfortable home may occasionally break the law, but they do not account for the explosion of violence that threatens our society.

Rather than seeking to prevent crime by creating a society based on the principle of inclusion, we have been driven to a war against those who have been excluded. In the course of fighting this war, we have abandoned one after another of the core values that formerly defined our society. Law enforcement has been degraded by the use of informers, entrapment, and paid witnesses. The Fourth Amendment's protection against unreasonable searches and seizures, the Fifth Amendment's guarantee of a fair trial, and the Sixth Amendment's assurance of the right to defense counsel have all been compromised by the U.S. Supreme Court under pressure to "win the war." Vague and sweeping catch-all laws have been passed, such as the federal RICO statute, which would have surely been deemed unconstitutionally broad by an earlier and more independent Supreme Court. A single crime can be multiplied into many offenses at the discretion of prosecutors, greatly increasing the penalties. Most defendants never get a trial, but are intimidated into pleading guilty by lack of funds to defend themselves plus the threat of much heavier punishment if they insist on a trial.

Many defendants cannot afford a lawyer, and those lawyers who serve as appointed defenders have shockingly insufficient financial resources to conduct an adequate defense. Recent laws allow the prosecution to seize the assets of the defendant in advance of trial, including the money needed to pay for a defense. Asset-seizure laws have become a potent temptation to corruption because the seized assets, including automobiles, boats, and homes, may then be used by law enforcement agencies, giving them a pecuniary motive for overreaching. Undercover informants are paid to entice people into committing crimes for which they can then be arrested. Large sums of money are paid to prosecution witnesses for their testimony, and witnesses are also promised leniency in their own cases in return for testifying the way the prosecution wants. Stephen B. Bright, director of the Southern Center for Human Rights, has documented how poor defendants in death penalty cases are often assigned totally inexperienced, incompetent, and sometimes even intoxicated lawyers for their defense.[6]

The majority of judges today are selected from the ranks of prosecutors rather than from the broader legal community, and few defense lawyers are ever chosen for the bench. Judges in federal courts are required to follow rigid mandatory sentence guidelines which leave no room for the administration of justice on an individual basis. Politicians frequently blame "judicial leniency" for increased crime, making it very difficult for any judge, elected or appointed, to conduct a truly fair trial.

By far the largest factor in the current crime wave is society's campaign to outlaw the sale and use of addictive drugs, a problem that could have been handled as a public health issue comparable to the use of alcohol and tobacco. Drugs are the painkillers of the poor, the jobless, the excluded—the inmates of the outside prison that our inner cities have become. By criminalizing the efforts of the poor to obtain relief from daily misery, we have created much of the crime wave we so greatly fear.[7]

The goal of this entire deplorable criminal process is punishment. Punishment takes the form of imprisonment—for longer and longer periods of time and under conditions that have grown steadily worse as overcrowding and cutbacks on care have made prisons into places of cruelty and horror. Incarceration today often means suffering repeated rapes and sexual assaults by other prisoners. The prison authorities do nothing to stop these attacks, which reportedly number in the hundreds of thousands annually. Outside of prison, rape and sexual assault are considered heinous crimes. Inside, they are part of the punishment. If a judge said, "I sentence you to be sexually assaulted on a daily basis" it would be plainly unconstitutional. Yet that is exactly what judges are sentencing many prisoners to endure—without taking responsibility for doing so. Overcrowding, neglect of prisoners' health, and the failure to prevent violence by prisoners against other prisoners have become de facto forms of punishment which could never pass constitutional muster but continue because the U.S. Supreme Court has cut off almost all avenues by which prisoners can have their rights adjudicated. And many prisoners suffering this form of unconstitutional punishment have not all been convicted of any crime. The Supreme Court has approved "preventive detention"—a flagrantly unconstitutional practice—of a growing number of persons, including juveniles, who are awaiting trial and may well be found innocent. Sometimes an accused person spends several years in prison only to be found not guilty—but this person has been punished and perhaps irrevocably damaged nevertheless.

California has the questionable distinction of operating perhaps the most dehumanizing prison yet invented. At Pelican Bay prison in Northern California, an institution for the "worst" of California's huge prison population, inmates suffer a "living death" of total isolation, kept in stifling heat, never seeing the sun, never breathing fresh air, fed through slots in the steel door to their cells, monitored on video panels, receiving commands by loudspeaker.[8] At a federal court hearing over harsh conditions at Pelican Bay, lawyers representing the inmates said that the extreme isolation in windowless eight-by-ten-foot cells for all but ninety minutes each day drives inmates crazy.[9] They are all but literally buried alive.

Nowhere in America—not in the sheltered confines of a university, not on a mountaintop or on a beach, not in a movie theater or restaurant or at home under the blankets in bed—is it possible to escape from

the awful knowledge that fellow human beings are con-
tinuously suffering under inhuman conditions. If we
shut this knowledge out, if we deny that it affects us,
then we in turn become victims of dehumanization.

If our American gulag held political prisoners, or
members of a persecuted religious or racial minority,
or dissenters and free-thinkers of any kind, then everything would look different to us. If the inmates of our
prisons were seen to be like the victims of Soviet or
Nazi tyranny, then in an instant the image of our country would change along with our self-image. Everything depends upon whether or not such mass
incarceration of human beings is justified. If they deserve their suffering, then we are still a "good" country
and each of us can enjoy a clear conscience. If their
suffering is preventable by a change in the economy,
then our cherished country has become a major viola-
tor of human rights and we are all burdened by that
fact in everything that we think and do.

We should not fail to observe that the System
gains a lot from crime. The System needs an enemy
now that the cold war is over. The criminal threat of
today serves much the same purpose as the Commu-
nist threat of yesterday. Crime supports a huge growth
of "big government," including a national law enforcement apparatus the framers of the Constitution never
contemplated and the "prison-industrial complex" that
sees prison-building as a form of economic growth.

The next logical step—the "privatization" of prisons as money-making business enterprises—is already well underway.

The wrongs of the System are kept from public debate by yet another large-scale wrong—suppression of free speech by domination of the channels of communication. Today we have the form of free speech but not the substance the framers intended. Instead of a debate, we hear only one side. Loss of genuine free speech has resulted from corporate control of all mass media plus the ability of employers to limit the speech of employees. Corporations use their financial leverage to magnify their views and to silence the views of others. Their control over speech was accomplished by several steps which have largely remained invisible to the people. We need to follow this story with care.

In 1886, the U.S. Supreme Court made a major and radical change in the nation's charter. The Court held that corporations were "persons" entitled to certain of the rights and protections given to individuals by the Constitution and the Bill of Rights.[10] This decision, which was reached by a Court that did not even hear argument on the issue and cited no basis for its "interpretation," was revolutionary in its application to free speech. A corporation uses other people's money to achieve great market power. To say that a corporation may also use other people's money to achieve massive power in the marketplace of ideas drastically reduces the power of individuals to govern society by adding a class of super-citizens with whom ordinary citizens cannot compete. The very idea of super-citizens defeats the essential premise of democracy that all individuals are politically equal.

Mass media such as television diminish the freedom of individuals to communicate—not by direct censorship (the individual can still stand on a street corner and attempt to speak to passersby) but by swamping, by drowning out, by denial of access to an audience. Few people realize that all television and radio channels belong to the public, not to networks, not to major corporate station owners, not to advertisers and sponsors. These channels were supposed to be allocated by the Federal Communications Commission in a way that served the "public interest." Channels could have been widely distributed among a diverse array of groups and interests in society. In fact, the channels were given to large corporate interests, especially those which already controlled newspapers or other important media outlets.

The corporate advantage over individuals in the competition to be heard is greatly magnified by the startling fact that corporate expenditures for advertising, including advertisements which express political or social views, such as the Mobil "op. ed." ads in newsmagazines and newspapers, are tax deductible as business expenditures. This means that the public is forced to subsidize the corporate viewpoint, while at the same time the efforts of individuals to be heard are not tax deductible.

In recent decades corporations have used their tax-deductible money to influence opinion and dominate thought in many new ways. First, massive funds were channeled into "think tanks"—supposedly independent (and tax-free) "foundations" which employed scholars to develop and disseminate a pro-corporate, pro-System philosophy. Second, funds were used to endow teaching positions in the nation's leading universities and professional schools, as well as for academic journals and conferences. Third, articles produced by corporate think tanks were made available to the influential op-ed pages of the nation's leading newspapers. Fourth, corporate funds were used to sponsor a whole series of talk shows and news analysis shows on television, including public television, where the regular panelists were almost all conservative in outlook, the guests were often supplied by the same think tanks, and those with anti-System views were almost totally excluded from appearing. Fifth, the corporate foundations also supplied funds for the preparation of pro-System articles and books. Sixth, corporate money was channeled into the campaign funds of elected officials such as members of Congress, especially through the PAC device, ensuring that more and more pro-System individuals of both parties would be returned to elective office. Seventh, commercial advertising on television, and in newspapers and magazines, increasingly endorsed not merely consumer products but also pro-System ideas along with the products. Sponsors would pay for an endless series of "pro-police" programs but not for programs stressing constitutional liberties.

Jerome L. Himmelstein writes that beginning in the 1970s, big business began to mobilize all of its resources "to support policies it deemed in its interests: cutting tax rates on profits and investment income, defeating labor law reform, preventing the creation of a consumer protection agency, limiting the growth of government domestic spending, and promoting deregulation of specific industries. . . . They threw their wholehearted support behind a conservative economic agenda. . . . Most important, big business mobilized in a hegemonic way. . . ." Business presented a united front "not only to influence specific pieces of legislation but also to shape policy discussion and formation generally in a way congenial to big business."[11]

The final stage in closing down individual free speech has been the use by corporations of their authority over the workplace: The millions of citizens employed by corporations as well as by government find that their right of free speech is subordinated to the employer's right to command. The U.S. Supreme

Court has been particularly assiduous in upholding employer power over employee speech. In a recent decision, *Waters* v. *Churchill* (May 31, 1994), an obstetrics nurse in a public hospital had a conversation with another nurse during a dinner break in the hospital cafeteria. Churchill, the nurse, criticized the hospital's policy of allowing nurses from one department to work in another department when staff shortages occurred, because the reassigned nurses lacked the training necessary for departments other than their own. The conversation was overheard by another employee who reported a disputed version of it to a supervisor, and Churchill, an employee for several years, was dismissed for comments deemed "non-supportive of the department and its administrative leadership." The Supreme Court made clear that an employee's speech is not protected if the employer believes that the speech might interfere with the efficiency of the employer's operations. "When someone who is paid a salary so that she will contribute to an agency's effective operation begins to do or say things that detract from the agency's effective operation..." her speech may be punished by dismissal. Of course, after losing her job, Churchill remained "free" to speak up on any issue.[12]

During the recent health-care debate, IBM sent a memo to its 110,000 workers urging them to contact their senators and representatives to urge defeat of bills proposed by Senator George Mitchell and Congressman Richard Gephardt.[13] Apparently employees do retain their free speech rights so long as they support their employer's views.

Today, instead of free speech, we have the carefully coordinated use of all of the media and the organized intellectual prowess of the country to create and maintain an official picture of reality which serves as the basis for the System's domination. As long as we believe, for example, that even the largest corporations are "private" enterprises subject to a "free market," or that the legions of the unemployed could find work if only they tried harder, basic change will remain out of reach. It is this false map of reality which must be challenged in order to oppose the System with any hope of success.

5

A
NEW MAP
OF
REALITY

Ａs the destruction caused by the System continues, there will inevitably be a new wave of protest, comparable in many ways to that earlier age of protest—the sixties. But this time protest must find a way to be effective, to unite rather than divide, and to achieve a change of direction. Sincere but misdirected gestures must be replaced by a strategy that works. The stakes are much higher now than in the sixties, for we are closer to the brink of nonsurvival.

We must ascend from spontaneous protest to intelligent opposition. Protest is directed at particular wrongs. Opposition seeks to change the System itself. Unlike protest, opposition requires a correct diagnosis of what is wrong and a believable vision of how things could be better. Opposition will provide a great learning experience for Americans.

Comparisons of protest then and now can be helpful and important. In the nineties, protest will not be

limited to youth or to students—the elderly will protest; people whose jobs are endangered will protest;
there will be protests on behalf of children. Tangible
economic issues such as health care, the minimum
wage, and job security will be heard of more frequently
than broad abstractions such as "alienation" and "dehumanization." Protest will be better focused; such di-
visive issues as the Vietnam War and the draft will not
be present to cause confusion.

Professor Edward P. Morgan has summarized the
sixties democratic vision as follows:

> (1) *equality*, or the full inclusion of soci-
> ety's dispossessed;
>
> (2) *personal empowerment*, or the libera-
> tion of each person from psychological con-
> straints as well as social oppression—a shift
> from masculinist "power over" to the femi-
> nist "power to";
>
> (3) a *moral politics* grounded on belief in
> individual growth, compassion for one's fel-
> low human beings—indeed for all life—and
> intolerance of injustice; and
>
> (4) the central importance of *community*
> as a locus for meaningful engagement in life
> and politics.[1]

Protest in the nineties will retain these core values, but
there will be a new emphasis on correcting the destruc-

tiveness of the economic system, healing the conflicts that are tearing America apart, plus structural and institutional change to accompany personal change. Protest in the nineties will avoid the mistake of appearing to be opposed to reason; instead, the chaos and irrationality of the System will be emphasized. And nineties protest will avoid the mistake of appearing to be anti-American, and instead will seek to reclaim the original idea of America from its usurpation by the System.

For the nineties as well as for the sixties, the most difficult challenge concerns the means of change. Professor Barbara Epstein, a historian of the sixties, concludes that the greatest weakness of that period's protest movements was lack of strategic thinking about how to accomplish its goals.[2] The System has effectively blocked the normal channels, such as elections, by forcing voters to choose between candidates who offer equally unpalatable programs and outlooks. Offered only a choice between evils, the voter is helpless. Likewise the whole constitutional system of checks, balances, and government under law has been largely superseded by the System. But this does not mean that change is impossible or that we are truly powerless. It means only that we need a new theory of change.

Although the System possesses all the means of social control in the arsenal of a modern state, including a monopoly of force, the System has come to rely more and more on a unique means of rule that it has developed: the control of "reality." By shaping and limiting our knowledge and our thinking, the System causes us to fight the wrong enemies and prevents us from seeing or even imagining better alternatives. In order to combat this form of rule, successful opposition must mount a challenge to the System's version of reality.

Ideas are vitally important, but a simple battle over ideas will not succeed. The System has been able to transform ideas into something far more powerful—pictures or models of reality. The "free market" is not merely an idea but a picture. The "private sector" is another picture. The "welfare mother," the "predatory criminal," and the "big government bureaucrat" are also ideas transformed into pictures. By this method, an entire ideology can be rendered as a series of pictures making up a comprehensive map of reality. Constantly repeated without rebuttal or dissent, these pictures and the map they form set the parameters of debate and imagination. Even dedicated liberals and reformers fall into the trap of seeing reality in the way the System portrays it. If we are menaced by predators or paranoids, then it follows that we must defend ourselves by abandoning constitutional safeguards and building still more prisons. On the other hand, if we were shown instead a picture of damaged and desperate people, a very different remedy would be called for.

The power of ideology turned into pictures was

recognized sixty years ago by Thurman Arnold in his seminal work, *The Symbols of Government*. Arnold described the new science of "image projection": "The thinking man with principles of the past generation has gone out the window; principles have no place in the science of image projection."[3] Arnold's insights were carried further by Daniel J. Boorstin in *The Image*. In his Introduction, Boorstin says: "In this book I describe the world of our making, how we have used our wealth, our literacy, our technology, and our progress, to create the thicket of unreality which stands between us and the facts of life."[4] He summarizes his conclusions: "Nowadays everybody tells us that what we need is more belief, a stronger and deeper and more encompassing faith. A faith in America and in what we are doing. That may be true in the long run. What we need first and now is to disillusion ourselves. What ails us most is not what we have done with America, but what we have substituted for America. . . ."[5]

Since the time of Arnold and Boorstin, the creation of false pictures of reality has been undertaken with ever greater success by corporate-sponsored think tanks and talk shows. Ian Mitroff and Warren Bennis write: "Unreality is big business. It involves the expenditure of billions of dollars annually. It is deliberately manufactured and sold on a gigantic scale. The end result is a society less and less able to face its true problems directly, honestly, and intelligently."[6]

To understand the immense power of ideas once they have been transformed into a map of reality, let us consider the "insoluble" and "intractable" problem of poverty. According to the System, there are no known solutions. A *New York Times* reporter writes:

> If anyone knew for sure how to lift people out of poverty, Americans would embrace the solution eagerly. It would make everyone's life safer and more prosperous.
>
> But no one does know, and no one has known since people first started thinking and talking about the problem in biblical times.[7]

As a *Los Angeles Times* article puts it, this view "symbolizes the ascendancy of the perspective that affixes blame for poverty primarily to self-defeating and self-destructive behavior by the poor"—a problem beyond the power of society to remedy.[8] Both Republicans and President Clinton apparently share the view that only moral renewal and "personal responsibility" can uplift the poor.

This picture of reality should be compared with the view of Louis D. Brandeis, quoted in chapter 2, that poverty is caused by the concentration of wealth and disappearance of jobs engendered by giant corporations. In 1933, Senator Hugo L. Black proposed a thirty-hour workweek. Speaking of the nation's 12 million unemployed, Black asked, "Have we not taken away from them the security that comes from honest work and honest toil and an honest job?" Black pointed out that burdensome overwork is forced upon others at the same time that millions are deprived of any work at all. "[T]he time is ripe for recognizing the fact that people, human beings, are the things that need to be protected in this country. . . ."[9]

Today, a similar senseless condition of overwork for some together with unemployment for others exists. Professor Juliet Schor, like Senator Black, sees no solution "without an equalization of the distribution of work itself."[10] Today, this practical solution to poverty has simply been excluded from the prevailing map of reality. Instead of maldistribution of work, we are shown only a picture of people who are to blame for their own inability to find employment. Thus poverty becomes insoluble. The prevailing map of reality fails to show that there is a nationwide and indeed a worldwide crisis of unemployment. The very word "depression" has been eliminated from the economic vocabulary.[11] In this area, as in so many others, ideology has become "reality."

Protest and opposition, whatever form they take, can succeed only by challenging the prevailing view of reality. The task of opposing the System demands that we learn to see the world around us independently of the pictures pressed upon us by the System. As the art historian Bates Lowry has pointed out, seeing is very different from merely looking. "We are not born with a knowledge of how to see. . . . Looking and seeing are as different as babbling and speaking. . . . Seeing is an act that occurs only with effort; we must train ourselves to see."[12] What Lowry says concerning art is even more true of perceiving the physical and economic world. Accordingly, the indispensable tool for opposing the System is a new map of reality.

The existing map has been very carefully developed. It consists of a series of views, pictures, and models supposedly depicting our world. Each view is like a picture with a caption. The caption interprets the picture just as a caption does on a newsphoto or as a descriptive title does on a map. The "views" themselves cover many areas, from the "geography" of society to the impact of the economy.

The best way to challenge this map is to analyze it frame by frame, construct an opposing map, also frame by frame, and if possible try to imagine some views of the unexplored territory outside the System, where a better way of life may be possible. These three sets of views—Existing Map, Opposing Map, Map of New Territory—will show us that we have a wide choice of views where reality is concerned. Every view, from whatever map, represents an idea—an idea about reality. These ideas are immensely powerful. By coming to recognize them we can gain access to their power.

We turn first to the ideas about reality found in the existing map. These are pounded into us day by day. Nevertheless, we gain power by being able to name, articulate, and criticize the ideas we are being subjected to.

EXISTING MAP

1. SHORT NARRATIVE. We are living under the best possible economic system. Our troubles come from excessive individualism and excessive government, both of which developed in the sixties. We must continue to advance technologically, while at the same time returning to an earlier form of personal behavior, culture, and government. There is no contradiction between going forward in one area (technology, economic organization) and at the same time attempting to return to the past in another area (behavior, government).

2. PUBLIC SECTOR, PRIVATE SECTOR. America is geographically divided into two sectors, "public" and "private," with "public" referring to government. By dividing America into these two sectors, we are given a view of reality where the private individual and the giant corporation are considered to be alike. All distinctions between the personal zone of individuals and the organized zone of corporate power are wiped out. The word "private" is used to include both the personal and the corporate. "Private" corporate power is made to seem totally different from public government. "Bureaucrats" who work for the government are denounced, but this criticism apparently does not apply to bureaucrats who work for an airline, a bank, or a telephone company. In addition, the fact that much corporate power is closely interlocked with public government is obscured. Most important, public—private dichotomy creates the illusion that Jeffersonian "freedom" is to be found outside the reach of public government. The existence of a deepening conflict between the interests of individuals and the interest of "private" corporations is rendered invisible.

3. ALL MAY RISE IN THE ECONOMY. This includes several subviews: (A) There is room inside the economy for all who want to work. (B) The work of any adult is exchangeable on the free market for enough money to supply the needs of a family in contemporary America. (C) Position in the economic hierarchy is determined by a fair competition based upon merit and hard work. (D) Those who fall into poverty failed to take advantage of opportunities open to them.

The belief that it is possible for every person to rise as high as he or she deserves is based on the myth of an unstructured economy with jobs and opportunities for all who earn them. This myth is perpetuated by describing the "private sector" as a zone of freedom and equality, rather than a zone where individuals confront private economic power. If it is true that all may rise, then poverty and inequality—even extreme inequality—are the result of the natural forces of competition among human beings.

4. THE ECONOMY IS BASED UPON A FREE MARKET. The image of the "private sector" as a zone of freedom is further supported by describing our economy as a "free market" rather than a carefully managed system with restricted opportunity. The market image suggests free and equal individuals exchanging handmade shoes for homegrown geese in a village square. This bucolic picture carries with it the notion that a job is just an individual contract between equals. Markets are said to possess a wisdom that is somehow superior to human wisdom. Indeed, this idea of the "market" has been raised to a sacred status equal to democracy itself. The free-market image prevents us from questioning decisions that are made and paths that are chosen by fallible human beings.

5. ECONOMIC GROWTH IS UNIVERSALLY BENEFICIAL. Economic or social ills cannot be due to any negative effects of growth, and an explanation for these ills must be sought elsewhere—in human failings or governmental interference.

6. GOVERNMENT HAMPERS GROWTH. The less public government the better, despite the presence of an economic machine that takes governmental actions affecting the entire nation. According to this view, public government can be local even when the economy is national. Any growth of government is deemed bad, but any growth of giant corporations is considered good.

7. EVERYTHING ESSENTIAL TO HUMAN LIFE CAN BE MEASURED IN "ECONOMIC" TERMS. Whatever lacks "economic value" may be disregarded, including the natural environment, the human habitat, and human needs for such "noneconomic" values as justice, security, and trust.

8. INDIVIDUALS CAN SUPPLY THEIR OWN NEEDS WITHOUT GOVERNMENT HELP. The less people pay in taxes, the better off they are, according to this view. People can presumably supply their own clean air, pure water, interstate highways, and open spaces.

9. INDIVIDUALS NEED NO PROTECTION FROM THE ECONOMIC SYSTEM. Continuing the free-market myth, we do not need protection against unsafe working conditions, impure food and drugs, banks that fail, or the refusal of employers to bargain fairly with employees.

10. RESPONSIBILITY SHOULD BE IMPOSED ON INDIVIDUALS BUT NOT ON ORGANIZATIONS. Under this view, the law should make it easier to punish individuals but more difficult to hold corporations guilty of wrongdoing. Workers or consumers injured by corporations should be limited in the amount of compensation they may receive, because large judgments add to the costs of doing business. This illustrates the broader tendency to deny the existence of costs or else to impose costs on those who lack political and economic power.

11. WELFARE AND ENTITLEMENTS ARE HANDOUTS. According to this view, individuals who are forced to give up control of their livelihood to centralized managers receive no protection or compensation in return. The economic

machine has no reciprocal responsibilities to individuals. If the System fails to provide some individuals with an opportunity to earn a living,
then it owes them nothing. Welfare and entitlements are merely a do-good effort by government
to "make life better." Worse, according to this
view, welfare represents a "redistribution of
wealth" from productive members of society to
the unproductive. The opposing view sees a very
different redistribution of wealth: from those who
are excluded by the economy and denied the value
of their labor to those who are fortunate enough
to have a paying job or other sources of wealth
within the System.

**12. WELFARE RECIPIENTS SHOULD BE
REQUIRED TO WORK.** This view overlooks the
fact that welfare came into being because there
were not enough jobs for those who needed them.
Today the shortage of jobs continues, even for
those with college degrees. Requiring work when
there is no work is a cruel and hypocritical use of
a false map of reality.

**13. SOCIAL PATHOLOGY SUCH AS POV-
ERTY AND CRIME RESULT FROM PER-
SONAL MORAL FAILURE, NOT ECONOMIC
DEPRIVATION.** On April 6, 1995, Robert Mac-

Neil interviewed House Majority Leader Dick
Armey on The "MacNeil-Lehrer NewsHour."
Their conversation included the following:

MACNEIL: I noticed you wrote recently, in the
Christian Science Monitor, that the Great Society mis-diagnosed poverty, as a material,
rather than a moral phenomenon. Can you
explain that? How do you explain poverty as
a moral phenomenon?

ARMEY: Well, there's no doubt about it. First
of all, it is the strength of our character as
individuals that is in fact the way we make
our way in life. If in fact we do not learn the
skills of adult responsibility because in fact
we have been taken care of and not allowed
that opportunity to do that, we are destined
to remain dependent on other people. And
the fact of the matter is, the Great Society ba-
sically said, Let's put our faith in the strength
of government, not in the strength of the
character of real people . . . we will put you so
thoroughly under the care and feeding of the
federal government that you can never learn
the skills of independence and freedom. . . .

MACNEIL: How do you distinguish between
that—what you just outlined—and saying
that means that people are responsible for

their own poverty and the old sort of idea that they should pull themselves up by their own bootstraps?

ARMEY: Pulling yourself up by your own bootstrap is not an experience alien to America. You can go into any community you want, including the halls of Congress, and find people that have come from any number of different and varied disadvantaged backgrounds, that have put their shoulder to the wheel, that have sort of deliberately exercised their independence and their ability, demanded that they be evaluated, judged on their own merit in life, and move forward. These are skills that we learn. . . .

MACNEIL: So you're going to teach America to do this?

ARMEY: We will let America be more free to teach their children, as America will, because America is a nation of loving parents.[13]

14. WE ARE BECOMING A NATION OF WHINERS. An illustration of this view is Charles J. Sykes's book *A Nation of Victims: The Decay of the American Character*.[14] This view is a way of making people blame themselves for grievances and thus abandon the quest for reform.

15. THE TWO POLITICAL PARTIES REPRE-SENT A FULL SPECTRUM OF VIEWS. The terms "left," "right," and "center" have altogether lost their original meaning. The original "Left" (a term for those advocating a socialist form of society) no longer exists. Those to whom the term "left" is now applied represent the former "center." What is now called the "center" would have been the "right" not long ago. The importance of this terminological legerdemain is that it preserves the appearance of a competitive political system offering genuine choice when in fact there is little or no significant difference between Democrats and Republicans.

16. NO ESSENTIAL CHANGE. This view insists that despite the passage of two hundred years, there has been no essential change in our nation's structure; everything that the framers of the Constitution intended still functions in the same way today. Hence common sense is all that is needed to fix everything, and no new ideas are needed to govern the radically changing economy of the nineties.

The foregoing views are just a few of those that compose the Existing Map. For contrast, we need a set of views in which the same underlying conditions are interpreted in a way that opposes the System and supports greater claims on behalf of human beings and nature. The power of such an Opposing Map lies in the fact that it creates a debate about reality, where no such debate now exists. The views in the Opposing Map provide a sampling of the unheard side of that much-needed debate.

OPPOSING MAP

1. SHORT NARRATIVE. The problems of American society have been accumulating for many decades, during which the System has increasingly failed to serve the interests of the nation as a whole. The sixties involved efforts to respond to these problems at both the governmental level (war on poverty) and the personal level (efforts to get beyond the economic). Our problems do not stem from a lack of personal responsibility, but rather from the avoidance of responsibility by the System.

2. UNACKNOWLEDGED SOCIAL CHANGE. Where the Existing Map sees no essential change since 1776, the Opposing Map sees vast change, much of it unacknowledged, that must be taken into account if we are to understand and govern our world.

3. MANAGERIAL ECONOMY. Major decisions are made by a centralized group of corporate and governmental managers rather than by the operation of Adam Smith's "Invisible Hand." A managerial economy is morally different from a free market because the individual's economic fate is controlled by others who thereby incur responsibility for their exercise of power. For example, the extent of poverty is determined by managerial decisions over which the poor themselves have no control, such as interest rate increases that diminish the number of available jobs.

4. PUBLIC-PRIVATE MERGER. Talk of "the private sector," of "privatization," and of aversion to "big government" assumes a boundary between "public" government and corporate government that no longer exists. There has been, for all practical purposes, a merger between what is still called "the public sector" (all forms of government—national, state, local) and what is still called "the private sector" (corporate). Both are equally "bureaucratic"; it is absurd to rail against government "bureaucrats" but not against corporate "bureaucrats."

5. THERE IS NO "FREE MARKET." Our economy utilizes markets, but they are carefully controlled, not free. As any working person knows, the large employer controls the labor market. Adam Smith would not have recognized nor approved of today's so-called markets.

6. STEEP PYRAMID. Society is shaped by the System into a pyramid with a few excessively privileged and powerful people at the top and a huge vertical drop to the bottom where people lead lives of deprivation and desperation. This shape is in contrast to the expectation after World War II that America would become a country with a large and prosperous middle class and no extreme contrasts between rich and poor. The Steep Pyramid is responsible for extreme inequality, which destroys community and threatens society.

7. POLITICAL V. ECONOMIC LIBERTY. The Framers assumed that if political liberties, such as the right to vote, received protection, economic liberty would not require protection. But conditions have changed, and today, economic liberty and political liberty can no longer be separated. Without economic liberty, there is no political liberty. In F.D.R.'s famous phrase, "necessitous men are not free men."

8. CONTROL OF LIVELIHOOD. Our ideas of economic freedom are based on the premise that we each control our own labor as a source of livelihood. When conditions change so that a job becomes the only possible source of livelihood for most people, and when jobs are tightly controlled by a small group of large employers, the individual loses the economic basis of independence and freedom.

9. POWER AND PAY. Under the System, pay is determined not by the value of one's work to society but by the power one has in the System's hierarchy. Teachers are poorly paid even though their services are essential to the future of society. Members of Congress and CEOs are well paid because they fix their own salaries. Work is drawn away from where it is needed and toward areas where power predominates.

10. EMPLOYMENT AS A RELATIONSHIP. A job is not merely an economic arrangement; it is also a personal relationship involving such values as trust, commitment, fair dealing, and mutual respect. The employee cannot avoid these issues, because they are part of what is expected under the term "work." But the employer can and frequently does fail to reciprocate. For example, employers think nothing of laying off workers after years of loyal service. This lack of mutuality in the employment relationship is a cost imposed on workers and on society. Despite denials, lack of commitment by employers to employees is a causal factor in lack of commitment by individuals to families.

11. WORKPLACE RIGHTS. We need to recognize the conflict between the authoritarian workplace and democratic values. Workers are discouraged from learning the habits of citizenship. Moreover, the workplace is largely exempt from the Bill of Rights. Free speech means little if the penalty is losing your job. This is the dilemma we face without workplace rights.

12. DISMISSAL AS REJECTION. Employers who dismiss longtime employees for economic reasons maintain that there's "nothing personal" in the dismissal. This leaves an injury that the employee must bear without compensation. Dismissal registers emotionally as a painful rejection and loss of place in the community. Such dismissals are a frequent cause of violence as embittered former employees return to inflict often fatal harm on supervisors or anyone else at the workplace.

13. SURPLUS PEOPLE. Instead of talking about an "underclass" we should be talking about a growing class of surplus people who through no fault of their own are unneeded by the economic machine. Since this is a worldwide problem in all industrial nations, the effort to place blame exclusively on the unemployed individuals is without justification.

14. RESPONSIBILITY GAP. The "paranoia" of paramilitary groups and others who express hatred and fear of the government is fueled by the fact that large organizations, and especially governments, are adept at avoiding responsibility when they cause harm. One of the great modern "inventions" is the avoidance of personal responsibility by use of the organizational form. Corporations were expressly designed to limit the liability of investors, and all bureaucracies, "private" as well as public, create such a long chain of command between the initiator of a policy and the person who carries it out that if harm or even death occurs, responsibility is avoided by all participants.

15. AMORAL GROWTH. Economic growth can be completely amoral. Growth may be based on the sale of harmful products, such as guns; it may represent the growth of social pathology, such as the building of more and more prisons; it may benefit a privileged few while further impoverishing many. Economic growth can and often does accompany a loss of values and morality if these do not "pay" for themselves. Economic growth is as consistent with authoritarian regimes and exploited labor as it is with democratic institutions.

16. DEPLETION. This word should be as familiar as "economic growth" and as frequently used in economic discussions. It refers to the impoverishing side of what we call growth—the unpaid costs of growth.

17. UNMEASURABLE COSTS AND VALUES. Many of the most important social values and costs, such as trust and the loss of trust, have no price tag and cannot be measured. As a result, they are undervalued or ignored in economic calculations, and are readily subject to depletion. For example, among the many "intangible" or "unmeasurable" costs of economic progress, loss of security is one of the greatest. People are expected by the System to live with more and more insecurity. But there is no evidence that human beings are able to tolerate this degree of uncertainty. Likewise, beauty and ugliness have no price tags, but their impact on human happiness or despair is profound.

18. IMPOSED COSTS. When workers are laid off to increase the employer's profits, the individual workers and their families are forced to bear all of the costs of joblessness rather than having these costs allocated among stockholders, other investors, upper-level management, customers, and the public. Costs are borne by those with the least power rather than by those who continue to receive profits and income.

19. ROGUE COSTS. Costs that are unacknowledged tend to surface in unexpected ways where they are all the more damaging because they are out of control. If we fail to acknowledge industrial pollution as a cost, then it is free to damage both the natural environment and human beings. Because we deny the existence of a cost we frequently ascribe its consequences to some other source and therefore lose the ability to control the damage being done. If we really want to do something about "fatherless families," for example, we should recognize loss of family unity as a cost of reduced employment opportunities, especially for young fathers. A society that supports fathers by making decent jobs available is more likely to pro-

mote family integrity than a society that confines
its efforts to moralistic preachments.

20. GROSS DOMESTIC COST. We now measure our national well-being by compiling a figure called "Gross Domestic Product." However,
GDP is misleading because it omits many kinds of
costs and losses which should be deducted from
growth. A society could gain a more accurate picture of its well-being by compiling and publiciz-
ing a figure called "Gross Domestic Cost," which
would make us aware of costs and losses. Such a
list might include:

- depletion of natural resources
- loss of open space
- pollution of air and water
- youth unemployment
- crime and violence
- neglect of children
- family abuse and breakup due to unemployment
- extreme inequality
- substance abuse
- fear, insecurity, and psychological depression
- underutilization of human abilities

This list could be extended indefinitely, and huge
dollar amounts could appropriately be attached.

For example, a figure of several hundred billion dollars could be assigned to crime if we included imprisonment, the cost of security, loss to victims, and more. Such a figure dwarfs the cost of providing every unemployed person with a good job. Two hundred billion dollars would pay for eight million jobs at $25,000 each.

21. NEED DEPRIVATION SYNDROME. More and more people seem to be human time bombs, suddenly losing control and committing acts of senseless violence. Whenever this happens, the media invariably sum up their reports by asking "Why?" In order to answer this question, we must invent a concept such as Need Deprivation Syndrome. Human beings have a remarkable ability to endure many specific deprivations, but the massive deprivation of many needs sends the individual into shock. Isolation, loneliness, rejection, loss of a job can drive one person to suicide and cause another to become suicidally violent. This is one of the unrecognized costs of an economy that is indifferent to basic human needs.

22. THE OUTSIDE PRISON. In the nineteenth century, being disconnected from the organized sector meant freedom, because new opportunities beckoned. More recently, being disconnected from the organized sector means having no money and possibly no home, lacking the means to be free. The total lack of freedom that accompanies poverty on the "outside" helps to explain why the threat of imprisonment often fails as a deterrent. Too many individuals in our society have nothing to lose.

23. ECONOMIC DEATH. In an earlier time, getting fired was a part of life that most people could survive and even joke about. Today, especially for those in middle age, it can mean economic death. People who lose their means of support, their home, and their ability to obtain the necessities of life are not simply "poor" or "unemployed" or "homeless"—they are not surviving. This is worth remembering when we read about profitable companies laying off thousands of workers so that the wealth of investors can be increased.

24. CRIMINALIZATION. This is a process by which society actually creates more crime by passing laws criminalizing behavior previously deemed permissible. Some actions, such as murder, are always considered criminal. Other actions, such as manufacturing, selling, and consuming alcoholic beverages or drugs, may or may not be considered crimes, depending on what laws are passed. When previously lawful behavior is criminalized, society creates its own "crime wave." Criminalization increasingly serves as a way of dealing with surplus people.

25. US V. THEM. This is a view of social conflict in which one "side" is dehumanized, treated as "the enemy," and subjected to exclusive blame for conditions which are also the responsibility of others. The common humanity of all groups in society is denied, and warfare replaces a search for the common good.

The Opposing Map makes possible a debate where none has existed for many years. So long as only one side is heard, its mythology remains unchallenged no matter how outrageous. Thus the absurd proposition that welfare causes poverty has been repeated by Republicans and Democrats alike in total disregard of history and the worldwide disappearance of jobs. The origin of this myth in corporate-funded think tanks has also gone unchallenged, although the self-serving nature of the myth is apparent the moment it is pointed out. An Opposing Map is essential to democratic dialogue.

The power of a set of connected ideas was demonstrated in the 1994 election. Starting with a small group of intellectuals, the neoconservatives, a set of ideas was created and disseminated with astounding political success. The 1994 election was a triumph of these ideas, not of individual candidates. A single idea—that government is "too big"—was enough by itself to win over millions of voters. And this idea was joined with other ideas providing additional power—for example, the idea of personal but not corporate responsibility.

Meanwhile, it has repeatedly been said that liberalism has no ideas. We hear that liberalism is exhausted, that it represents the failed solutions of the past. Why is the liberal larder so empty? The answer is that neoconservatism has made effective use of the Existing Map, and those who speak for liberalism do not challenge the map itself. For example, liberals fully accept the gospel of growth and the fantasy of the free market. Liberals have no new ideas, because they are confined within the narrow walls of the Existing Map.

The power of the Existing Map is immense, yet the power of ideas from the Opposing Map is potentially far greater. If liberals or others, whatever their label, would start using just one idea from the Opposing Map, they would be back in business, they would have the System on the defensive, and they would gain access to a bountiful harvest of fresh thinking. For example, anyone who seriously wants to change the course of this society could simply start saying "There is no free market." Without the free market, we would have to take responsibility for the choices that create so much unnecessary economic hardship. We could ask the System to explain why it perpetuates poverty and the neglect of children given the enormous, sky-rocketing social costs of doing so—costs that are over-whelmingly greater than what it would cost to give everyone a place at the table and a decent start in life. Without the myth of the free market, the present choice would be difficult or impossible to defend.

Ideas that support the System are forcefully re-peated day after day in all the media by the most au-thoritative voices available, from the president of the United States on down. But if *there is no free market* received even a modest airing, the effect would be transformative. People would want to know who makes the decisions formerly ascribed to the free mar-ket, and how can these decisions be justified. Those who want to defend expenditures for education, for child nutrition, for cleaning up our rivers could all strengthen their causes by saying *there is no free market*.

Now suppose we added a second idea, *responsibility gap*, and put as much power into its dissemina-tion as has been put into *personal responsibility*. This would open a debate about whether responsibility is only personal, or whether responsibility also accompa-nies the exercise of economic power, and whether responsibility is increased by reason of the possession of power over other people's lives.

The "new" idea that the economy must be managed in the best interests of society as a whole, and that to do otherwise is irresponsible, is alone capable of changing the direction in which the country is heading. If everyone from environmentalists to victims of racial and other forms of discrimination, from opponents of the war on crime to advocates for the elderly were all to take up the cry of *there is no free market, responsibility gap,* they would have the System on the defensive.

The power of ideas from the Opposing Map is enhanced by the degree to which they have been suppressed. The opposing ideas have the power of the fresh and new after the endlessly repeated tedium of the old. But their greatest source of power is that the present choices made by the System will lose in any open and fair competition with choices based on the best interests of society. How can it possibly be rational to neglect the education of our children, to pollute our air and water, or to destroy our natural beauty?

Suppose the opponents of the System were to make use of a third idea—Gross Domestic Cost—so that, in every debate with proponents of the System, we were exposed to *there is no free market, responsibility gap, Gross Domestic Cost.* The false account books used by the System would be exposed. The tiresome chant of "deficit reduction" would be rendered irrele-

vant by the exposure of our social and human deficit,
the neglect of our land and people, which is the true
cause of our impoverishment. Our task would then be
seen not as fiscal conservatism but as the conservation
and replenishment of our natural and human resources.

But the greatest power of opposing ideas is that
they open the way to a vision of something beyond our
present imagination. They allow us to see our present
predicament as due to the tyranny of narrowly defined
economics. The Opposing Map tells us that we are required to take a historic step beyond the economic.

Freedom from economic tyranny means that we
are not always forced to make choices dictated by economics. We could choose to spend more time with our
children, choose work with greater social value, choose
caring for others as a profession without unreasonable
financial sacrifice. We lack this necessary freedom not
because of tyranny by government—the form of tyranny best known in 1776—but because of tyranny by
economic power.

Consider the fundamental issue of whether there
are decent work opportunities for all who seek them.
Economic tyranny dictates that there be a permanent
surplus of those seeking employment. The larger interest of society is that work be available to all who need
it. This is a choice we must confront. We have avoided
making this choice by believing that economic growth

will automatically produce jobs. But in fact growth has recently been based on reducing both the quality and number of jobs. We need to decide which is more important: economic rationality or having everyone belong to the economic community. Economic tyranny precludes us from making this choice. We should, for example, be able to compare the cost in economic efficiency of providing everyone with a job, with the cost of an angry underclass of surplus people. With greater freedom of choice, we might decide that the latter cost is far, far greater. But however we choose, we need to know that it *is* a choice and that we, rather than nameless forces, are responsible for the consequences.

Most of the important things in life, the things we truly desire, such as love, joy, and beauty, lie in a realm beyond the economic. What we do not recognize is how economics has become the destroyer of our hopes. It is economic tyranny that cuts off our view of a better future. When we try to look ahead now, we see only a shrinking world, with less of the things we really want at higher prices and in exchange for harder, less meaningful work. This is an accurate vision of where economic tyranny is taking us.

The present split between the economic and the noneconomic, with the economic holding almost all the levers of power, is a historical anomaly that cannot be sustained. Ideally, the "economic" should include all of life, as it once did. There would be nothing wrong with a society based on the economic if "economic" were defined broadly and inclusively. But as the definition of "economic" has narrowed, more and more essential aspects of life—and more and more members of society—are excluded. If the raising of children, the support of community, and the development of human character and potential are excluded from the "economic," as they now are, the result will inevitably be a society torn apart by conflict and impoverishment despite a "flourishing economy."

We need to see that our present situation is not an act of God but entirely self-composed, and we need to see that other choices are available. For example: Suppose we decided that the value of including everyone as a meaningful participant in society's work outweighed the economic inefficiency of doing so. (We have, after all, decided the opposite, with catastrophic results.) There is nothing to prevent us from organizing our society to include all. Perhaps the economic machine would be slowed down and would produce less of what is now defined as wealth. But we would simply be exchanging one kind of wealth for another.

Today, we annually produce a miraculous crop of fresh young people filled with hope, nobility, and the desire to show what they can do. We then condemn the vast majority to unrewarding and often meaningless work far below their abilities and potential—work that will drain them and bury their dreams. We condemn a large group to total exclusion and rejection.

Suppose we chose instead to give up some of what we presently call wealth in exchange for wealth in another form. We could then offer every young person a chance to perform work that would be a source of pride, dignity, and fulfillment. Our new wealth would consist of living in a society with greater happiness and satisfaction, where much more human energy was utilized to benefit society, and where we would be surrounded by more attractive and available human beings. At the same time, many of society's worst problems would be healed in time. Is this such an irrational choice? Does our present choice of wasting so much human possibility and disappointing so many hopes for the sake of economic efficiency make sense? We are fortunate that we are free to make a different choice.

The alternative to the present economic tyranny is a society based on fundamentally different philosophic principles: balance—perhaps a fifty-fifty proportion between the economic and the noneconomic—and choices made by the conscious decision of the people rather than by managers relying on impersonal economic forces. Such a society could return us to the promise of abundance and expanding freedom that has been all but abandoned in favor of scarcity and repression.

The principle governing an alternate, or "posteconomic" society would be the maintenance of a balance between the human environment and the material economy, a division of energy and resources between the two, with the object of preventing and resolving the kind of conflicts that are now tearing us apart. Historically, we have expected our economic system to maintain such a balance under the guidance of Adam Smith's "invisible hand." But the noneconomic depends upon altruism, sacrifice, and a willingness to forgo income that most people cannot afford. And Smith's capacious idea has degenerated into a narrowly defined concept of the market that excludes too much.

In making a major effort to preserve and maintain a human environment on a par with the material economy, we would be achieving several goals essential to the success of any human society. First, we would preserve a space for individuals to perform those functions which must be performed by persons rather than by organizations—child raising, for example. Second, we would recognize that human beings are biological entities, not machines, who have needs which must be met, such as the need for security. Third, we would enable people to develop the independence, intelligence, responsibility, and knowledge to enable them to perform their role of citizens who can give orders to the System. Fourth, we would provide an unlimited supply of challenging and fulfilling work for those who are underemployed or not needed at all by the material economy. Fifth, we would enable people to construct strong enough supports for their lives so they could practice the virtues and become the creators that are so needed today.

We can choose to protect a personal sector against the pressures of the economy. The personal side of life requires *time*. There is no way, for example, that a relationship with another person can be created and maintained except by an investment of time. But personal time must be protected against the demands of the workplace, which has the urgency of economic necessity. We can choose many other "noneconomic" values. Serious people have argued that contact with nature is not a mere amenity, but an essential ingredient in character formation, in mental health, and in human happiness. If so, then more parks and wilderness might be a factor in making it unnecessary to construct more prisons and mental hospitals. Today, we starve and neglect our natural resources of all kinds—for the sake of some other form of wealth. Even when an area is saved from development and set aside as parkland, it is more and more likely to be overcrowded and understaffed. We could allocate five or ten times the resources to nature than we do now, to balance the increasing urbanization and computerization of society.

Investment on so grand a scale of course raises questions of feasibility. If we have no money now, where would it come from? We should try to imagine

the enormous savings that would be possible if we reduced existing conflicts. *Business Week* estimated the
cost of crime alone at $425 billion a year.[15] The cost of
poverty may be greater still. And the cost of extreme
inequality may exceed both. Conceivably, more than
half of all the wealth we now produce is wasted in
order to pay for the repression of social conflict. None
of this wealth is available to enhance life in a positive
way. And even the remaining part of our wealth is not
fully enjoyable in the midst of so much conflict. So we
could be better off in every respect if we chose to enjoy
a better balance in the forms of wealth.

If we want to change society, we must change
ourselves into a new version of citizenship. We must
place ourselves in a position both outside and above
the System. We must rise to a level where We the People dominate the machine. We must be able to criticize
and reject its "reality." We must be able to command
the managers to serve us, and not merely themselves,
or be dismissed. We must reject the model of economic
man and the rule of so-called economic forces. The
only way to dominate the machine is to be smarter
than the machine.

Citizenship today presents far greater problems
than citizenship in the eighteenth or nineteenth cen-
turies. Today's citizen cannot possibly know or understand as much about particular issues. Government
and society have reached a degree of complexity that

only the insider can fathom. Today's citizen is more like a shareholder of a giant corporation. We each have a big stake and a big investment in the national economy. Such a citizen-shareholder-consumer is excluded from the inner workings of the System, and must therefore vote or make choices based upon *results*.

Based on results rather than ideology, the System would deserve a vote of no confidence. The result that matters most is the well-being of the people who make up this society. If there is a marked increase in violent crime, the System should be held responsible. It should matter not at all that the System has an anticrime program, or that the System proclaims a war against crime. From the citizen's point of view, it is the result that counts, and the bottom line is that there is more crime, not less. No matter how loudly senators and congressmen proclaim they are against crime, the citizen should hold them responsible for the fact that crime is on the rise. Whatever they may say, these legislators have proven to be pro-crime, because that is the bottom-line result of their stewardship. For this they should be fired. If there is more unemployment, more poverty, more addiction, and more family breakdown, the System and its managers should be held responsible and dismissed no matter how much they say they are against these evils. After all, this is the rule of responsibility in the corporate world. If a manager fails to make a company profitable, he will be fired regardless of how loudly he proclaims that he is "pro-profit" and regardless of his "pro-profit program." Likewise, if citizens find they are not better, happier, healthier, those in power must be held responsible for these results, not their posturing and promises.

In judging results, the citizen must not be beguiled by anything short of an improvement in people. Military triumphs, budgetary victories, space exploration, patriotic observances may stir enthusiasm, the president's ratings may rise, but the citizen must remember that all of our scientific and material creations are only means, not ends. Nothing produced by the five hundred largest corporations has any meaning apart from the life of human beings. Nothing done in law, medicine, government has any meaning apart from human beings. Buildings may rise hundreds of feet, jets may circumnavigate the earth, spacecraft may penetrate the outer reaches of the solar system and enter the universe beyond, but none of this means anything except in relation to human beings.

The System is a machine. If we allow it to do so, the System will continue to dominate us all. It makes little difference which party we vote for, or who the president is, if our leaders are subordinated to the machine. It makes little difference what we believe, if our beliefs are formed from the conventional wisdom served up on television, in the newspapers, and in the newsmagazines by the machine. The fact that we passively ratify what is being done does not make us citizens, but rather the manipulated subjects of machine domination.

Because the System has so effectively suppressed criticism of itself, many people do not know that, in formation, the System was profoundly questioned by leading Americans of an earlier time, some of whom believed that the coming of the System would mean the end of American democracy. Franklin D. Roosevelt warned repeatedly that the nation must establish "practical controls over blind economic forces and blindly selfish men"; that technology without moral controls would be "a ruthless master of mankind."[16] In a later message, Roosevelt told Congress that "The first truth is that liberty is not safe if the people tolerate the growth of private power to the point where it becomes stronger than that of their democratic state itself. That, in its essence, is Fascism. . . ."[17]

There is a great contrast between a society where a person is valued only as a machine part, trained for this limited purpose only, discarded when no longer useful to the machine, and a society where people are the ultimate product and the more they are cultivated the richer society becomes. Under the System, we have come dangerously close to believing in the first model, forgetting all that a person can be. The waste of human capacities and powers in our society is so great that we rarely catch even a glimpse of human potential. Paul

Goodman saw this trend forty years ago: "[T]here get to be fewer jobs that are necessary or unquestionably useful; that require energy and draw on some of one's best capacities; and that can be done keeping one's honor and dignity."[18]

Under the System we have forgotten that the whole point of democratic society is to produce better people, not better things.

In 1939, the philosopher John Dewey wrote:

> The ultimate problem of production is the production of human beings. To this end, the production of goods is intermediate and auxiliary. It is by this standard that the present system stands condemned. . . . Machinery and technological improvement are means, but again are not the end . . . the means have to be implemented by a social-economic system that establishes and uses the means for the production of free human beings associating with one another on terms of equality.[19]

The idea that human beings are what matter and an economic system is just a machine provides the starting point for a third map of reality—a map that shows the territory outside and beyond the System, as well as how to get there. The central point is that our problems *can* be solved. Poverty, crime, the destruction of habitat and environment all stem from a single underlying cause—economic tyranny—and the solution lies in a society that is *posteconomic*. A detailed program must be the work of future generations. But some of the essential steps that must be taken are an appropriate part of a Map of New Territory. Once the artificial walls of the Existing Map no longer block our vision, we should be able to see a long way in every direction. Instead of a future where hopes are extinguished, we should see the unlimited possibilities that really do exist beyond and outside the System.

MAP OF NEW TERRITORY

1. A PROGRAM. Neither of our political parties nor any independent candidates so far offer a program that attempts to go forward rather than backward. In the coming years such a program must be created. Initially, it might include:

2. WHAT IS AN ECONOMIC SYSTEM FOR? The economist Stuart Chase pointed out the vital importance of asking this question. We have the power to design a system that will do whatever job we ask of it. We are not limited to the models of the past.

3. REGAINING CONTROL. Citizens do not have to choose between "working within the Sys-

tem" and violent revolution. "Regaining control"
represents the middle ground of subjecting the
System to democratic authority. "Regaining control" is an appropriate concept in dealing with a
machine.

4. CONSTITUTIONAL RENEWAL. We should
amend or reinterpret the Constitution to take account of the many structural changes that have
occurred since 1789. The Constitution and the
Bill of Rights should be made applicable to economic or private government and to the workplace. Corporations should lose their special
status as "persons" and their ability to dominate
the political process and the channels of communication. Both the human habitat and the
natural environment require specific constitutional protection. Economic rights for individuals should be guaranteed along with political
and civil rights.[20] Changes such as these are required to restore the original vision of a society
where all governmental power is subject to law.
These changes would recognize the need to
bring private economic power under the Constitution and thus ultimately under the control of
the American people. New rights—for example,
to clean air, pure water, and decent housing—
are required because many individuals cannot
provide these needs on their own.

5. A NEW SOCIAL CONTRACT. We must revise the social contract to reflect the central role of organized economic power and to define the responsibilities that accompany such power. What interests must the managers represent—investors only or the public as a whole? Is there an obligation to provide economic opportunity for all who seek it? Are there limits to the economic inequality that society can tolerate? How can the autocratic nature of private economic government be reconciled with democratic ideals? The actual "contract" is a fiction, but its terms can be expressed in legislation or in constitutional provisions. Without such a revision of the social contract, there is a profound responsibility gap that allows the holders of the greatest power over the lives of ordinary people to escape the responsibilities of that power, leading directly to the discontent and anger of today.

6. HUMAN V. ECONOMIC DEVELOPMENT. The "wealth" which the economic machine is designed to produce must be redefined to make decent jobs and meaningful work as important a form of wealth as goods and services. Such an economy would attempt to preserve a fifty-fifty balance between the development of human beings and the development of their material surroundings. The alternative, in which work is stripped of meaning for many of those who have jobs, while others are entirely without jobs, is already becoming an impossible burden for society. Absent a basic reform of the economy, job training perpetuates the illusion that jobs are "out there."

7. REPLENISHMENT. A second great shift in the economy is needed to direct our work and energy into restoring the personal sector, where much of the damage caused by the System has occurred. All of the forms of caring for others should carry the prestige and economic rewards of work. Child care and help for the elderly should be well paid. A shift to the labor-intensive tasks of the personal sector will dovetail well with a commitment to provide meaningful work to all who seek it. There is an unlimited amount of "people-work" that needs to be done to reverse the damage of recent decades. Only this kind of effort will restore character, morals, values, and the other human qualities so noticeably lacking in American life; it is impossible to expect that the restoration of character and community will take any less massive an effort than was required for their destruction. To prevent this destruction from happening again, there should be an affirmative search for all the hidden costs that our economy generates, rather than the present ethic of hiding and denying costs wherever possible.

8. POSTECONOMIC. A more general shift in the economy is required in order to recognize that an economic system must be subject to the laws of nature and the biologically determined needs of human beings and a human community. The definition of economic value should be expanded to include the unmeasurables and intangibles that represent essential values that cannot be reduced to monetary terms. Family life, spiritual life, nature, health, trust, safety, and security are all intangible and unmeasurable but essential to survival. Unless they are assigned value in our economic system, they will be plundered, and efforts at preservation will fail to do any more than slow the destruction. We need a "posteconomic" society in which the major conflicts that have torn apart our society, such as the conflict between economic progress and preservation of the human and natural habitat, would be mediated rather than driven to extremes.

9. REDEFINING SELF-INTEREST. All of these changes must be brought about, not by governmental command but by the choices of individuals, acting separately but in concert, to shift our political and economic system toward greater control and balance. The dismal experience of socialism and communism proved only that centralized economic commands do not work; it did not prove anything about the ability of people to make new choices on their own, based upon a shared concept of self-interest. Our millions of individual choices can be effective agents of social change. And in the process, democracy can be reinvigorated.

10. RESTORING CITIZENSHIP. We need to restore citizenship by returning to the ideal of democratic individualism as described by Emerson, Thoreau, Whitman, John Dewey, and others in this tradition.[21] If the people are to govern, they must be capable of governing, and capable as well of resisting appeals to conformity from the mass media or from institutions and associates. We cannot expect to control the System unless we can place ourselves at an intellectual level above the System, where we can see the infinite other possibilities of life as well. In a society where organization possesses so much power to change individual behavior, individuals must be much more conscious of their species and evolutionary role, so that we can guide our own changes rather than submit to being changed by impersonal forces. We should try, as individuals and as a society, to escape the walls of ideological thinking and see society in a detached and scientific way as a practical means for human beings to live together.

11. SOCIAL PROTECTION. The above program reinstates a truth recently forgotten: Individual human beings require protection from the impersonal actions of any large-scale economy, as well as from the global economy. "Protectionism" should be a good word, not a bad one.

12. CITIZEN-SHAREHOLDER. The above program also assumes that an individual today must be regarded not only as a citizen but as a shareholder—meaning that society has in many ways become a business enterprise as well as a political arrangement. Everyone has a stake in this enterprise, and people should expect at least a minimum share.

13. SOCIAL SELF-KNOWLEDGE. Our society's greatest problems arise from mistakes concerning reality. A citizen's first responsibility is to have adequate knowledge about our society and economy so as not to be subject to manipulation and to be able to make choices consistent with the good of society. This is a task for educators and journalists and for citizens themselves. Given social self-knowledge, a person located anywhere inside or outside the System can navigate with sufficient accuracy to make decisions with awareness of their impact on society.

14. FREEDOM AS A PRACTICE. The System would have us believe that we are "free" even if we do nothing. But freedom is like physical fitness—it is an activity which must be practiced in order to exist. It may include both thinking and action, but it is not enough to say, "I could do (or think) something if I wanted to," any more than it is enough for an indolent person to say, "I could exercise every day if I wanted to."

15. ABOVE THE SYSTEM. From a point of view within the System, it seems as if the System is the only possible reality, that there is no "outside" or alternative. From a viewpoint above the System, such as a historian or anthropologist might take, we can see that many different systems are possible, and that beyond the System's walls a whole unexplored universe awaits us. Tennyson wrote: "Our little systems have their day; They have their day and cease to be."[22]

Experimenting with different maps of reality makes us realize that we human beings live in a world almost entirely of our own making. Nothing except the limits of our own imagination prevents us from making up a better world if the present one no longer serves us well. There are no "laws" of economics or politics except the laws of nature, and they should be respected more, not less.

While human beings have expanded their horizons in many directions, the mythology of politics and economics has remain trapped in the past, held there by the weight of the status quo. Just as we can travel in space or explore the structure of genes, we can also prevent violence and crime, reduce inequality, eliminate poverty, and endow work with the dignity and security that it deserves. All of these goals are actionable. None are beyond our present knowledge and resources. And since they are actionable, it is profoundly immoral for us to allow the present unjust and destructive order to continue.

The System is not America. It is not the "land that we love." It does not merit our loyalty, affection, or respect. However much the System may attempt to disguise itself in patriotic trappings, or set itself up as a source of authority, or cloak itself in the vestments of "the community," it is none of these. We should always be ready to fire the System if it does not serve us well.

It has been more than two hundred years since

human beings took their last great step toward liberty, when monarchy was replaced by constitutional democracy. The time has come for the next stage of human freedom: freedom from economic tyranny. Without this new form of freedom, our earlier freedoms cannot survive, because the economic now exerts far more power over our lives than the political. Freedom from economic tyranny must be to our era what freedom from monarchy was in 1776.

All of the territory beyond the narrowly economic is open to exploration and settlement. Opportunity is unlimited, because there are no limits to the forms of wealth that human beings can create in the realms of knowledge, culture, art, and expression. Our present loss of hope is a very recent phenomenon. Only forty years ago, in the 1950s, the world seemed filled with promise. Writing in the *Oberlin Alumni Magazine,* Geoffrey Blodgett, class of 1953 and professor of history at Oberlin, remembers:

> . . . we had the enormous good luck to believe that we possessed a desirable future. The society we were getting ready to enter seemed on balance to be a good society. Most of us were eager to find our places in its structure and fulfill ourselves in ways expected of us. . . . We thought we were needed by society, and by the professions we wanted

to pursue. The jobs were out there waiting
for us, slots to be filled. . . .

There seemed to be so much more within
the structure to reach for and achieve that
only an ungrateful fool . . . would try to reach
for things that could *not* be achieved. . . .
Then came the future we did not expect. . . .[23]

In the long view of civilization, we have made a
giant mistake. Making such mistakes is a privilege not
enjoyed by other life forms. If they make an evolutionary mistake, they die. But human beings have enough
leeway to make many mistakes, because we live far
above the survival level and because we can use reason
to correct our mistakes.

Opposition to the System requires a new consciousness. We must gain a point of view outside the
System. We must question the System's version of reality. We must assert authority over the System, hold it
responsible for the consequences of its decisions, impose democratic and constitutional limits on its uses of
power. We must recognize that our discontents and
conflicts will continue to increase until we overthrow
the tyranny of narrowly defined economic rule.

We have the opportunity and duty to serve our
species by restoring to human society the wholeness it
now lacks while creating a new abundance based upon
the development of human beings. Having been born

into a society that imposed an artificial reality upon us, we are free to make up whatever new reality will be of greatest benefit to all. Our institutions having failed us, we must rise to the challenge as individuals. In doing so we exercise our responsibility as citizens, create the next stage of human consciousness, and fulfill our duty as human beings to choose the upward path.

NOTES

EPIGRAPH

1. John D. Rosenberg, ed., *The Genius of John Ruskin* (Boston: Houghton Mifflin Co., 1963), p. 270.

2. THE INVISIBLE GOVERNMENT

1. Charles E. Lindblom, *Politics and Markets* (New York: Basic Books, 1977), p. 356.

2. *Liggett* v. *Lee* 288 U.S. 517, 542, 565 (1933).

3. *Liggett* v. *Lee* 288 U.S. 517, 580 (1933).

4. Jacques Steinberg, "At Wal-Mart, Workers Who Dated Lose Jobs," *New York Times*, July 14, 1993, p. A16.

5. Bruce Ackerman, "The Storrs Lectures: Discovering the Constitution," *Yale Law Journal* 93 (1984): 1013; Bruce Ackerman, "Constitutional Politics/Constitutional Law," *Yale Law Journal* 99 (1989): 453.

6. Thomas L. Friedman, "The Fear Is Old, the Economy New," *New York Times*, Sunday, May 22, 1994, Sec. 4, p. 1.

7. John Kenneth Galbraith, *The Affluent Society* (New York: Mentor New American Library, 3d ed., 1976), p. 221.

8. Ibid., p. 230.

9. Linda Davidoff, "Fields of Broken Dreams," *New York Times*, June 18, 1994, p. 21.

10. Theodore J. Lowi, *The End of Liberalism,* 2d ed. (New York: W. W. Norton & Co., 1979), pp. 25, 27.

11. Lindblom, *Politics and Markets,* pp. 238–39.

3. ECONOMICS V. SOCIETY

1. Alan Wolfe, *America's Impasse: The Rise and Fall of the Politics of Growth* (New York: Pantheon Books, 1981), pp. 30–31.

2. E.J. Mishan, *The Costs of Economic Growth* (New York: Praeger, 1967).

3. Paul Samuelson and William D. Nordhaus, *Economics,* 13th ed. (NY: McGraw-Hill, 1983), pp. 117–20.

4. Cass R. Sunstein, "Well-Being and the State," *Harvard Law Review* 107 (1994): 1303.

5. "8 Killed as Tour Plane Crashes at Grand Canyon," *San Francisco Examiner,* February 14, 1995, p. A10.

6. Susan Chira, "Study Confirms Worst Fears on U.S. Children," *New York Times,* April 12, 1994, p. A1.

7. G. Pascal Zachary and Bob Ortega, "Age of Angst: Workplace Revolution Boosts Productivity at Cost of Job Security," *Wall Street Journal,* March 10, 1993, p. A1.

8. Bob Baker, "Buyouts Batter the Workers," *San Jose Mercury News,* October 8, 1989, p. E1.

9. Stanley Meisler and Sam Fullwood III, "Tide of Want Has Millions Going Under," *Los Angeles Times,* July 15, 1990, pp. A1, A20.

10. Jane E. Brody, "Overcoming the Traumas of Losing Your Job," *New York Times,* March 25, 1992, p. C12.

11. Brendan Boyle, "Europe's Jobless Fight Boredom, Despair," *Los Angeles Times,* April 3, 1983, pp. 1A, 12, 14.

12. Al Martinez, "Laid-Off Workers Lose Pride, Trust, Not Just Wages," *Contra Costa Times,* July 26, 1991, p. 2A.

13. Jules Henry, *Culture Against Man* (New York: Random House, 1963), pp. 25, 26, 41, 42, 322–24.

14. Ashley Montagu and Floyd Matson, *The Dehumanization of Man* (New York: McGraw-Hill, 1983), pp. xiii–xiv.

15. "Boy Meets Girl, Boy Beats Girl," *Newsweek*, December 13, 1993, pp. 66, 67.

16. Lonnie H. Athens, *The Creation of Dangerous Violent Criminals* (Urbana: University of Illinois Press, 1992), p. 29.

4. THE GREAT LAWBREAKER

1. Tony Horwitz, "9 to Nowhere: These Six Growth Jobs Are Dull, Dead-End, Sometimes Dangerous," *Wall Street Journal*, December 1, 1994, pp. A1, A10, A11.

2. Campaign address on "Progressive Government" at the Commonwealth Club, San Francisco, California, September 23, 1932.

3. "A National Service Law and an Economic Bill of Rights," January 11, 1944, in Russell D. Buhite and David W. Levy, *FDR's Fireside Chats* (Norman: University of Oklahoma Press, 1992), pp. 282–93.

4. Robert H. Frank, "Talent and the Winner-Take-All Society," *American Prospect*, Spring 1994, p. 97.

5. Linda Greenhouse, "Justices to Take Up Case on Schools' Drug Testing," *New York Times*, March 29, 1995, p. A10. On June 26, 1995, the court upheld the school drug testing program in a 6–3 decision, with President Clinton's two appointees providing the deciding votes for the majority. Linda Greenhouse, "Schools Can Test Athletes for Illicit Drugs," *New York Times*, June 27, 1995, p. A1.

6. Stephen B. Bright, "Counsel for the Poor: The Death Sentence Not for the Worst Crime but for the Worst Lawyer," *Yale Law Journal* 103 (1994): 1835.

7. Steven B. Duke and Albert C. Gross, *America's Longest*

War: Rethinking Our Tragic Crusade Against Drugs (New York: Jeremy P. Tarcher/Putnam, 1993).

8. Nat Hentoff, "Buried Alive in Pelican Bay," *Village Voice*, June 22, 1993, pp. 20, 21; John Ross, "High-Tech Dungeon," *Bay Guardian*, September 23, 1992, pp. 15–17; Kevin Leary, "Pelican Bay State Prison—a Prisoner's Nightmare," *Sunday Oregonian*, July 7, 1991, p. E15; Nat Hentoff, "Pelican Bay Is Our Own Devil's Island," *Los Angeles Times*, December 5, 1993, p. M5.

9. Reynolds Holding, "Final Arguments in Pelican Bay Trial," *San Francisco Chronicle*, December 16, 1993, pp. A23, A26.

10. The background of the Court's 1886 *Santa Clara* decision is told in chapter three of Morton J. Horwitz's notable history, *The Transformation of American Law 1870–1960* (New York: Oxford University Press, 1992).

11. Jerome L. Himmelstein, *To the Right: The Transformation of American Conservatism* (Berkeley: University of California Press, 1990), pp. 130, 138–39.

12. *Waters* v. *Churchill* 114 S. Ct. 1878 (1994).

13. Glenn Rifkin, "IBM Urges 110,000 Workers to Help Defeat Health-Care Bills," *New York Times*, August 19, 1994, pp. A1, A13.

5. A NEW MAP OF REALITY

1. Edward P. Morgan, *The Sixties Experience* (Philadelphia: Temple University Press, 1991), p. 9.

2. Barbara Epstein, *Political Protest and Cultural Revolution* (Berkeley: University of California Press, 1991).

3. Thurman Arnold, *The Symbols of Government* (New York: Harcourt Brace and World, Harbinger Edition, 1962), p. ix.

4. Daniel J. Boorstin, *The Image* (New York: Atheneum, 1962), p. 3.

5. Ibid., p. 6.

6. Ian I. Mitroff and Warren Bennis, *The Unreality Industry* (New York: Carol Publishing Group, 1989), p. xii.

7. David E. Rosenbaum, "The Welfare Enigma," *New York Times*, February 10, 1995, p. A11.

8. Ronald Brownstein, "Welfare Debate Puts Blame for Poverty Mainly on Poor," *Los Angeles Times*, March 24, 1995, pp. A1, A22.

9. Hugo L. Black, speech to the Senate, April 3, 1933, reprinted in Howard Zinn, ed., *New Deal Thought* (New York: Bobbs-Merrill Co., 1966), pp. 263, 266, 267.

10. Juliet B. Schor, *The Overworked American* (New York: Basic Books, 1992), p. 151.

11. Wallace C. Peterson, *Silent Depression* (New York: W. W. Norton, 1994).

12. Bates Lowry, *The Visual Experience* (New York: Harry N. Abrams, 1961), pp. 13–14.

13. Interview with House Majority Leader Dick Armey, "MacNeil-Lehrer NewsHour," PBS, April 6, 1995.

14. Charles J. Sykes, *A Nation of Victims: The Decay of the American Character* (New York: St. Martin's Press, 1992).

15. "The Economics of Crime," *Business Week*, December 13, 1993, p. 72.

16. Kenneth S. Davis, *FDR: Into the Storm, 1937–1940* (New York: Random House, 1993), p. 41.

17. Ibid., p. 230.

18. Paul Goodman, *Growing Up Absurd* (New York: Vintage Books, 1956), p. 17.

19. John Dewey, "The Old Problems Are Unsolved," in Zinn, *New Deal Thought* (New York: Bobbs-Merrill, 1966), p. 413.

20. William O. Douglas, *A Wilderness Bill of Rights* (Boston: Little Brown & Co., 1965); Roderick Frazier Nash, *The Rights of Nature* (Madison: University of Wisconsin Press, 1989).

21. See George Kateb, *The Inner Ocean: Individualism and Democratic Culture* (Ithaca: Cornell University Press, 1992).

22. Alfred, Lord Tennyson, "In Memoriam A.H.H."

23. Geoffrey Blodgett, "An Apology for the 1950s," *Oberlin Alumni Magazine,* Spring 1982, p. 43.

INDEX

213